Peter R

CW00548154

Adapting Tolkien

Proceedings of The Tolkien Society
Seminar 2020

Edited by Will Sherwood

Copyright © 2021 by The Tolkien Society
www.tolkiensociety.org

First published 2021 by Luna Press Publishing, Edinburgh
www.lunapresspublishing.com

ISBN-13: 978-1-913387-69-3

Cover illustration *Vision* © 2021 Charlotte Cooper
Published under the auspices of the Peter Roe Memorial Fund, eighteenth in the series.

Contents

About the Peter Roe Memorial Fund

The Tolkien Society's seminar proceedings and other booklets are typically published under the auspices of the Peter Roe Memorial Fund, a fund in the Society's accounts that commemorates a young member who died in a traffic accident. Peter Roe, a young and very talented person joined the Society in 1979, shortly after his sixteenth birthday. He had discovered Middle-earth some time earlier, and was so inspired by it that he even developed his own system of runes, similar to the Dwarvish Angerthas, but which utilised logical sound values, matching the logical shapes of the runes. Peter was also an accomplished cartographer, and his bedroom was covered with multi-coloured maps of the journeys of the fellowship, plans of Middle-earth, and other drawings.

Peter was also a creative writer in both poetry and prose—the subject being incorporated into his own *Dwarvish Chronicles*. He was so enthusiastic about having joined the Society that he had written a letter ordering all the available back issues, and was on his way to buy envelopes when he was hit by a speeding lorry outside his home.

Sometime later, Jonathan and Lester Simons (at that time Chairman and Membership Secretary respectively) visited Peter's parents to see his room and to look at the work on which he had spent so much care and attention in such a tragically short life. It was obvious that Peter had produced, and would have continued to produce, material of such a high standard as to make a complete booklet, with poetry, calligraphy, stories and cartography. The then committee set up a special account in honour of Peter, with the consent of his parents, which would be the source of finance for the Society's special publications. Over the years a number of members have made generous donations to the fund.

The first publication to be financed by the Peter Roe Memorial Fund was *Some Light on Middle-earth* by Edward Crawford, published in 1985. Subsequent publications have been composed from papers delivered at Tolkien Society workshops and seminars, talks from guest speakers at the Annual Dinner, and collections of the best articles from past issues of *Amon Hen*, the Society's bulletin.

Dwarvish Fragments, an unfinished tale by Peter, was printed in *Mallorn* 15 (September 1980). A standalone collection of Peter's creative endeavours is currently being prepared for publication.

The Peter Roe Series

Abbreviations

A&I   *The Lay of Aotrou and Itroun*, ed. by Verlyn Flieger
                 (London: HarperCollins, 2016)

Arthur   *The Fall of Arthur,* ed. by Christopher Tolkien
                 (London: HarperCollins, 2013; Boston: Houghton
                 Mifflin Harcourt, 2013)

AW   *Ancrene Wisse* (Oxford: Oxford University Press, 1962)

B&L   *Beren and Lúthien*, ed. by Christopher Tolkien
                 (London: HarperCollins, 2017)

Beowulf   *Beowulf: A Translation and Commentary, together
                 with Sellic Spell*, ed. by Christopher Tolkien
                 (London: HarperCollins, 2014; Boston: Houghton
                 Mifflin Harcourt, 2014)

Bombadil   *The Adventures of Tom Bombadil and other verses
                 from the Red Book* (London: George Allen &
                 Unwin, 1962; Boston: Houghton Mifflin, 1962)

CoH   *The Children of Húrin*, ed. by Christopher Tolkien
                 (London: HarperCollins, 2007; Boston: Houghton
                 Mifflin Harcourt, 2007)

Exodus   *The Old English Exodus*, ed. by Joan Turville-Petre
                 (Oxford: Oxford University Press, 1982)

Father Christmas Letters from Father Christmas, ed. by Baillie
                 Tolkien (London: George Allen & Unwin, 1976;
                 Boston: Houghton Mifflin, 1976)

FoG	*The Fall of Gondolin*, ed. by Christopher Tolkien (London: HarperCollins, 2018).
FR	*The Fellowship of the Ring*
Hobbit	*The Hobbit*
Jewels	*The War of the Jewels,* ed. by Christopher Tolkien (London: HarperCollins, 1994; Boston: Houghton Mifflin, 1994)
Kullervo	*The Story of Kullervo,* ed. by Verlyn Flieger (London: HarperCollins, 2015; Boston: Houghton Mifflin Harcourt, 2016)
Lays	*The Lays of Beleriand,* ed. by Christopher Tolkien (London: George Allen & Unwin, 1985; Boston: Houghton Mifflin, 1985)
Letters	*The Letters of J.R.R. Tolkien,* ed. by Humphrey Carpenter with the assistance of Christopher Tolkien (London: George Allen & Unwin, 1981; Boston: Houghton Mifflin, 1981)
Lost Road	*The Lost Road and Other Writings*, ed. by Christopher Tolkien (London: Unwin Hyman, 1987; Boston: Houghton Mifflin, 1987)
Lost Tales I	*The Book of Lost Tales, Part One,* ed. by Christopher Tolkien (London: George Allen & Unwin, 1983; Boston: Houghton Mifflin, 1984)
Lost Tales II	*The Book of Lost Tales, Part Two*, ed. by Christopher Tolkien (London: George Allen & Unwin, 1984; Boston: Houghton Mifflin, 1984)

Monsters	*The Monsters and the Critics and Other Essays* (London: George Allen & Unwin, 1983; Boston: Houghton Mifflin, 1984)
Morgoth	*Morgoth's Ring*, ed. by Christopher Tolkien (London: Geore, 1993; Boston: Houghton Mifflin, 1993)
OFS	*Tolkien On Fairy-stories*, ed. by Verlyn Flieger and Douglas A. Anderson (London: HarperCollins, 2008)
P&S	*Poems and Stories* (London: George Allen & Unwin, 1980; Boston: Houghton Mifflin, 1994)
Peoples	*The Peoples of Middle-earth*, ed. by Christopher Tolkien (London: HarperCollins, 1996; Boston: Houghton Mifflin, 1996)
Perilous Realm	*Tales from the Perilous Realm* (London: HarperCollins, 1997)
RK	*The Return of the King*
Silmarillion	*The Silmarillion*, ed. by Christopher Tolkien (London: George Allen & Unwin, 1977; Boston: Houghton Mifflin, 1977).
Sauron	*Sauron Defeated*, ed. by Christopher Tolkien (London: HarperCollins, 1992; Boston: Houghton Mifflin, 1992)
Secret Vice	*A Secret Vice: Tolkien on Invented Languages*, ed. by Dimitra Fimi and Andrew Higgins (London: HarperCollins, 2016)

Shadow	*The Return of the Shadow*, ed. by Christopher Tolkien (London: Unwin Hyman, 1988; Boston: Houghton Mifflin, 1988)
Shaping	*The Shaping of Middle-earth*, ed. by Christopher Tolkien (London: George Allen & Unwin, 1986; Boston: Houghton Mifflin, 1986)
S&G	*The Legend of Sigurd and Gudrún*, ed. by Christopher Tolkien (London: HarperCollins, 2009; Boston: Houghton Mifflin Harcourt, 2009)
TL	*Tree and Leaf*, 2nd edn (London: Unwin Hyman, 1988; Boston: Houghton Mifflin, 1989)
TT	*The Two Towers*
Treason	*The Treason of Isengard*, ed. by Christopher Tolkien (London: Unwin Hyman; Boston: Houghton Mifflin, 1989)
UT	*Unfinished Tales of Númenor and Middle-earth*, ed. by Christopher Tolkien (London: George Allen & Unwin, 1980; Boston: Houghton Mifflin, 1980)
War	*The War of the Ring*, ed. by Christopher Tolkien (London: Unwin Hyman, 1990; Boston: Houghton Mifflin, 1990)

Introduction

Will Sherwood

'I would draw some of the great tales in fullness, and leave many only placed in the scheme, and sketched. The cycles should be linked to a majestic whole, and yet leave scope for other minds and hands, wielding paint and music and drama.' (*Letters*, 145).

'Here is a book very unsuitable for dramatic or semi-dramatic representation. If that is attempted it needs more space, a lot of space.' (*Letters*, 255).

These two epigraphs perfectly surmise Tolkien's conflicted views over the adaption of his work. One evidences him encouraging fellow creative minds to expand on his oeuvre, whereas the other contradicts and exposes his tendency to stand as the literal and figurative gatekeeper. His disdain for radio and film adaptions is well documented, as is Christopher Tolkien's dissatisfaction with Peter Jackson's film trilogies. Yet within Tolkien's life he encouraged adaptions such as Donald Swann's *The Road Goes Ever On* (1967) and Pauline Baynes illustrations, which he described as 'wonderful pictures with a touch of "fantasy"' (*Letters*, 312). These inconsistent notions have, however, failed to dissuade fans from reimagining Tolkien in a range of art and media forms. Tolkien has further come to be adapted into the very material of our universe.

Adaption as a mode is fundamental to the progress of art. Tolkien himself adapted styles, forms, language and tropes in order to create his legendarium – although within his wider context he was just one player in the Old English revival of the first half of the twentieth century. Indeed, within scope of the revival Chris Jones ranks him as the 'most popular poet of the twentieth century', achieving success and readership beyond that of his contemporary revivalists (13). His commonly ascribed title as the 'father of fantasy' is a further indicator of his work's impact. It is hard to read a Western fantasy novel published after *The Lord of the Rings* (1954 – 1955) without seeing its 'influence' as many modern Western fantasy writers have openly admitted their struggles in trying to escape Tolkien's shadow over the genre.

As this seminar proved, adaption extends far beyond the arts and into our own reality. The 'Frodo Lives!' counterculture slogan from the 1960s and 1970s evidences how Middle-earth seeped into and became a tangible element of our primary world very early on. And the pace has not slowed; in recent years names such as Strider and Gollum have been attributed to new discoveries of reptile fossils and subterranean fish.[1] Adaption further extends to Tolkien's fan-culture and readers. As was witnessed at the Diversity Panel at Oxonmoot 2020: how a reader visualises a character or environment can be in direct correlation to their background. This in turn has given rise to the *Alliance of Arda* initiative that seeks to challenge

[1]. See Ashley Strickland's article on the reptile fossil: https://edition.cnn.com/2020/04/08/world/mysterious-tolkien-ancient-reptile-scn/index.html and Josh Davis's article on the subterranean fish: https://www.nhm.ac.uk/discover/news/2019/may/new-species-of-subterranean-fish-named-after-the-lord-of-the-rings-character.html

established notions of who Tolkien belongs to and who his characters are, striving to unify fandom and encourage readings from those who feel 'under-represented'.

The Tolkien Society 2020 seminar, which took place on 4th of July, was unlike its predecessors as it was the first seminar to be held solely online. Its theme of 'adaption' was apt as the society had to modify the delivery of the seminar and other events that year. The online platform proved a staggering success as over four-hundred attendees and speakers from across the globe were welcomed on Zoom and YouTube. In order to accommodate as many time zones as possible, the event was condensed into a half-day seminar with ten papers and a panel discussion on the life and works of the late Christopher Tolkien, who had passed away early that year on 16th of January. Besides academic insights into existing adaptions, the seminar welcomed papers from two composers who had produced a significant number of musical adaptions of Tolkien's work.

Of the ten papers, six are presented in this proceedings. Cami Agan opens by situating Christopher as the inheritor and adaptor of his father's legendarium, arguing that he went beyond the role of 'editor'. Marie Bretagnolle follows by exploring the creative process behind Francis Mosley's illustrations for the Folio Society's *The Silmarillion*. Andrew Higgins starts to blend the visual with the auditory by examining how David Salo married together different versions of Quenya and Sindarin in order to provide mythic depth to Jackson's film trilogies. Brian Egede-Pedersen proceeds by guiding us on a journey through the realm of heavy metal. In particular, he brings to light Tolkien's presence and influence on the genre before focusing solely on the lyrics and discography of Battlelore. In the penultimate paper by Mina Lukić, the act of adaption is interlaced with the memory of the Professor. Lukić examines how individual, social, and cultural memory play central roles in the process of adapting Tolkien. Kristine Larsen concludes the proceedings with her mapping of Tolkien across the stars. Literally. Drawing on the International Astronomical Union's Rules and Conventions, Larsen explains how Tolkien's names have come to light up our night sky.

On behalf of the Tolkien Society, I would like to extend my deepest gratitude to the presenters of the Tolkien Society 2020 seminar, without whom the event would not have happened. I would also like to thank Anna Milon, Francesca Barbini, Dr Dimitra Fimi, the *Alliance of Arda* team, and the Society's committee for their continued support and guidance in the planning and running of the event, and the publishing of this proceedings. The publication itself is made possible by the generosity of the Peter Roe Memorial Fund, for which I am grateful.

Bibliography

About the Alliance, 2020, <https://allianceofarda.org/about-the-alliance/>
[accessed 2 January 2021].

Jones, Chris, *Strange Likeness: The Use of Old English in Twentieth-Century Poetry*, (Oxford: Oxford University Press, 2006).

Tolkien, J.R.R., *The Letters of J.R.R. Tolkien*, ed. Humphrey Carpenter (London: HarperCollins, 2006).

The First Age Materials:
Christopher Tolkien's Greatest Task

Cami D. Agan

Imagining Christopher Tolkien's task in the wake of his father's death reminds us of the enormity of his lifelong project: the extant documents "crammed in disorder in that formidable array of battered box-files" (*Peoples*, ix), a "fearsome textual jigsaw" with no clear order or chronology, and original drafts in pencil that were wholly erased and written over, often illegibly, in ink (*Lost Tales I*, 10). In his Preface to *The Silmarillion*, Christopher explains that in his first foray into the First Age materials, he aimed for a "coherent and internally self-consistent narrative" (8). With this goal, as he admits, Christopher at times went beyond the role of editor-compiler to adapter-author, when faced with competing versions of narratives and/or incomplete narratives in a sequence needed for the cohesion he sought. For example, Jason Fisher points out that Christopher's task involved "collecting, organizing, collating, editing, and even embellishing his father's scattered writings";[1] he goes on: "*The Silmarillion* might well have been full of poetry, as many of the underlying tales and legends . . . were composed in verse".[2]

---

1. Fisher, Jason, "From Mythopoeia to Mythography: Tolkien, Lonnröt, and Jerome", in *The Silmarillion Thirty Years On*," ed. by Allan Turner, (Zurich: Walking Tree, 2007), pp. 130-131.
2. Fisher, "From Mythopoeia," p. 122.

Fisher thus reminds us that readers' and scholars' first window into the Elder Days reflects Christopher's decision to prioritize this notion of a "coherent and internally self-consistent narrative" (*Silmarillion*, 8), adapting and even inventing where the manuscripts left him no choice. Of course, his emphasis on cohesion had roots in his father's wishes, who, after the completion of *The Lord of the Rings*, wrote of the Elder Days: "The legends have to be worked over . . . and made consistent; and they have to be integrated with *The Lord of the Rings*; and they have to be given some progressive shape. No simple device, like a journey or a quest, is available. I am doubtful myself about the undertaking" (*Lost Tales I*, 4). Perhaps no other testament to Christopher's achievement is greater than the fact that, despite his father's death, the disorganization of his unpublished materials, and the task of connecting them (or not) to the published Third Age works, he was able to succeed in giving us multiple portals into these "legends" in his father's stead.

Of course, *The Silmarillion* as published is now only one text of many giving us access to the Elder Days, thanks to Christopher's decades-long toil. Much of *Unfinished Tales*, as well as much of volumes 1-5 and 10-12 of *The History of Middle-earth* offer an immense wealth of detail about the First Age, including varying genres or modes, competing versions, authorial and editorial commentary, maps, linguistic detail, names, indices, genealogies, etc. These volumes, as Christopher explains in his preface to *The Peoples of Middle-earth*, grew from his own interest in his father's creative process; he undertook "an exhaustive investigation and analysis of all the materials concerned with what came to be called the Elder Days" (*Peoples*, ix). While there is substantial editorial commentary as to date of composition-revision, the condition of manuscripts, changes in narrative, etc., the controlling sentiment of cohesion or unity that so formed the published *Silmarillion* does not organize the *History of Middle-earth* texts. As a result, while these texts may ask more of readers, they provide a clearer sense of the way J.R.R. Tolkien worked through what Christopher calls "the vision of his vision" of the Elder Days (*Lost Tales I*, 7). Through these post-*Silmarillion* volumes, Christopher has revealed the "massive and continuous history" of the First Age and has consciously avoided attempts to reconcile competing strands of narrative (*Peoples*, ix).

Finally, the publication of *The Children of Húrin*, *Beren and Lúthien*, and *The Fall of Gondolin* offer up what Christopher calls his father's "Great Tales" of the Elder Days. In these volumes, Christopher hoped "to follow . . . one single particular narrative from its earliest form and throughout its later development" (*FoG*, 13). These volumes reveal the ways that Tolkien returned to the three great narratives again and again through his lifetime, intertwining them with the major thematics of the First Age, particularly the heroic-tragic-elegiac struggles of the exiled Noldor with the Sindar and Edain in Beleriand. For readers, even those familiar only with *The Hobbit* and *The Lord of the Rings*, it is easy to recognize the centrality of these great tales through the consistent allusions to them in later stories and songs.

In his roles as editor, executor, adaptor, and son, Christopher spent four decades fulfilling what he saw as his father's dearest desire: offering up the history and interconnected tales of the First Age. Together, *The Silmarillion*, the volumes of *The History of Middle-earth*, *Unfinished Tales*, and the three Great Tales reflect Tolkien's lifelong concerns with the themes,

9

histories, and narratives of the Elder Days. Likewise, the volumes all attest to and provide a foundation for the sense of an *existence* or *reality* to Arda's ancient past; they render the First Age a solidity in myriad ways through their various versions, frames, and interconnections. As a result of their multiple forms, competing strands, and ever-shifting names/ events, the ancient texts construct particular geographies, socio-political interactions, artifacts, languages and dialects, art and architecture, song and tale, borders and boundaries, journeys and maps, that now undergird any notion of Middle-earth or Arda, whether from a Primary or Secondary world perspective.

Indeed, as Christopher explains, the First Age materials as we now have them function on at least two levels: "in the history of Middle-earth the development was seldom by outright rejection – far more often it was by subtle transformation in stages, so that the growth of the legends . . . can seem like the growth of legends among people, the product of many minds and generations" (*Lost Tales I*, 8). Despite the challenge of making sense of his father's remaining manuscripts on the First Age, Christopher has managed consistently to provide us with a sense these two levels: the itinerary of his father's writing (and rewriting) process in the primary world, as well the sense of an ancient tradition for the inhabitants of the secondary world, Arda, of tales, histories, and other ancient texts saved from the wreck of Beleriand. He explains further: "my father as 'author' or 'inventor' cannot always . . . be distinguished from the 'recorder' of ancient traditions handed down in diverse forms among different peoples through long ages" (*UT*, 10). On one level, Tolkien, author and sub-creator, develops, expands, and revises the First Age materials from 1916 until his death; on another level, scholars and sages of Beleriand tell, retell, expand, recite and record legends from the Ainulindalë through the Great Tales of Beleriand, and central locales – such as Gondolin – become a repository for those tales, which then filter down through the ages in various forms. One of the crucial results of Christopher's life work, then, is his success in allowing access to these two conceptions of Arda, revealed particularly through the First Age materials.

To go further and provide a helpful way to consider these two resonances for the tales of the Elder Days, the notions of diegetic and non-diegetic serve to highlight the primary and secondary world divide.[3] In film, "diegesis" or the diegetic refers to any element within the world of the film. Diegetic sound, for example, refers to sounds, whether music or other ambient noise, that characters within the film can hear. The sound of Gimli blowing the horn at Helm's Deep, Éowyn's funeral dirge for Théodred, the explosions of Gandalf's fireworks at Bilbo's birthday party in Peter Jackson's *Lord of the Rings* films, for instance, are all diegetic, all part of the world of the film. On the other hand, non-diegetic refers to anything not a part of the world of the film that characters of the film cannot see or hear, but that audiences can: the score, the credits, internal monologue, Galadriel's narration of the events of the One Ring's forging that brings us to the opening of *Fellowship of the Ring*, for example. Considering the text from the reader's perspective – the legend-history in Tolkien's texts which render that world "more real" for the reader in

3. Mark J.P. Wolf offers an insightful exploration of narrative constructions with an emphasis on the diegetic, referencing *The Lord of the Rings* and *The Hobbit*, among many other texts. "More than a Story: Narrative Threads and Narrative Fabric," *Building Imaginary Worlds; The Theory and History of Sub-Creation* (New York: Routledge, 2012), pp. 198-225.

the primary world – emphasizes the non-diegetic, the effects on those outside the world of Arda. Likewise, examining the First Age materials with attention to the source material or composition, revision, and dating of Tolkien's works orients to their non-diegetic properties, how they function in or were crafted in the primary world.

From a non-diegetic perspective, for readers, having the First Age materials available results in an even greater sense of what critics such as Tom Shippey[4] and Michael Drout[5] have called the "depth" in Tolkien's work: the sense it gives us of layered history and the weight of reality we glimpse behind the world of Middle-earth. These references to past events and tales hearken to what Tolkien called the "body of more or less connected legend" in his sub-creation that readers see reinforced through allusion (*Silmarillion*, xii). Christopher, too, attends to readers' desires to know details of Middle-earth's history more fully. In his Preface to the *The Children of Húrin*, for instance, Christopher explicitly claims that "This book is thus primarily addressed to such readers as may perhaps recall" references in *The Lord of the Rings* to Ungoliant, Beren, and Túrin and wish to know more about them (*CoH*, 8). This dedication foregrounds the non-diegetic in that Christopher seeks to have these First Age allusions clarified for readers, for those of us in the primary world.

In fact, Christopher often grounds the forewards and prefaces to his edited volumes of his father's works with attention to the non-diegetic. For example, he alludes to his father's revision

---

4. Shippey, Tom, *The Road to Middle-earth: How J.R.R. Tolkien Created a New Mythology*, (Boston: Houghton, 2003).

5. Drout, Michael, and others, "Tolkien's Creation of the Impression of Depth." *Tolkien Studies*, 29 (2014), pp. 167-211.

process of the First Age materials: "it is to be remembered that 'The Silmarillion,' from the 1926 'Sketch' onwards, was written as an abridgement . . . giving the substance of much longer works (whether existing in fact, or not) in smaller compass" (*Lost Tales I*, 9). By locating us in a primary world date (1926), Christopher references his father's tendency to condense longer First Age works into a tighter scope, or at least hearken to the existence of longer works behind his Sketch of the Mythology. It appears a largely non-diegetic discussion, focused on Tolkien as sub-creator in process. Frequently in his letters, Tolkien likewise discusses the First Age texts as his own sub-creation and thus non-diegetically. For instance, his famous letter to Milton Waldman explains: "Behind my stories is now a nexus of languages . . ." (*Silmarillion*, xi); "my stories" thus positions Tolkien as maker of the world and the languages of that world (*Silmarillion*, xi). In a letter to Katherine Farrer, Tolkien notes that "These tales are feigned (I do not include their slender framework) to be translated from the preserved work of Ælfwine of England . . ." (*Morgoth*, 5). His explanation here points to his early construction of the tales of the Elder days, and through the term "feigned," Tolkien reveals himself as the ultimate maker or sub-creator in the non-diegetic sense (5). Although Christopher provides Tolkien's notes and addendums to the various versions of First Age materials as part of *Unfinished Tales* and the *History of Middle-earth*, Tolkien, once he abandons the Ælfwine framework, typically maintains a sense of these works as for the inhabitants of Arda, rather than making non-diegetic references to an outside reader or world.

In contrast, examining the First Age materials diegetically means to consider them as texts, manuscripts, and "compendious

13

narratives" (*Silmarillion*, 8) within the realm of Arda itself, as remnants of the lost libraries of Gondolin, tales brought from Valinor over the Grinding Ice, and salvaged and preserved in Imladris, for example. From this vantage, the surviving narratives – references, partial tales, even objects like Sting, "a blade made in Gondolin . . . of which so many songs had sung" (*Hobbit,* V, 65) – clearly have vital significance for those in Middle-earth. Christopher explains, for example, that "the tale of the Children of Húrin is integral to the history of Elves and Men in the Elder Days" (*CoH,* 10). Here, Christopher refers diegetically to the tale of Túrin, a tale which interweaves much of the downfall of Beleriand and its aftermath, with a focus on the significance of that tale – in whatever form – for the inhabitants of Arda. Likewise, he notes, "The tale of the Fall of Gondolin gathers as it proceeds many glancing references to other stories, other places, and other times: in the past that govern actions and presumptions in the present time of the tale" (*FoG*, 16). By emphasizing the "present time of the tale" (*FoG*, 16), Christopher grounds the Great Tale of Gondolin in the diegetic sense and points to the ways it is interlaced with other accounts both past and in the time of the First Age; he prioritizes a sense of the tale existing and interacting with other stories of the lost Beleriand.

Within the tales of the Elder Days themselves, the conscious sense of a frame or of tale-telling heightens the diegetic qualities of the texts, or suggests how those tales have proliferated and impacted the inhabitants of Arda. Consider the following passage:

> Among the tales of sorrow and of ruin that come down to us from the darkness of those days there are yet some in which amid weeping there is joy and under the shadow of death light

14

that endures. And of these histories most fair still in the ears of the Elves is the tale of Beren and Lúthien. Of their lives was made the Lay of Leithian, Release from Bondage, which is the longest save one of the songs concerning the world of old; but here the tale is told in fewer words and without song. (*Silmarillion*, 162).

As the opening paragraph of the chapter "Of Beren and Lúthien" in the published *Silmarillion*, the passage offers numerous diegetic layers: the narrative voice positions itself distanced in time from the events of the tale, as if looking back, suggesting its survival and importance through the ages in Middle-earth. "Among the tales of sorrow" reveals that there are many surviving tales of the Elder Days into later times; the reference to the 'Lay of Leithian' points to varying versions and genres of the same tale; "fair still in the ears of the Elves" reveals that the Free Peoples hearken to the First Age tales consistently and value the lives and actions of their ancestors (*Silmarillion*, 162). Finally, the self-conscious "here the tale is told in fewer words and without song" suggests the later inhabitants of Arda continually retell these vital stories in various forms, and even that the interior, diegetic narrator is familiar with, and may even be consulting, other manuscripts containing those versions (*Silmarillion*, 162).

As the above passage attests, the availability of the First Age materials reveals their crucial significance for inhabitants of Arda, and the ways in which the variety of texts – poems, discursive essays, partial narratives, competing versions, framing devices, etc. – unveil a tradition through which these inhabitants understand their ancient past. They have become cornerstones of cultural and personal identity for those within

Arda, bringing into high relief the themes through which those inhabitants construct meaning: exile, death/immortality, aesthetic creation, cultural cooperation. For characters in later times such as Bilbo and Frodo but even for Elrond, Aragorn, and Faramir, these tales and texts contain their history, genealogy, mythos, philosophy, art, even legal decision, and thus provide a sense of identity and connection to past places, events, and people forever lost. In one of the most famous passages in *The Lord of the Rings*, Sam and Frodo reflect on the ways their quest aligns with the ancient quest of Beren and Lúthien, and in the telling or retelling of that tale in brief, they find connection, hope, and the ability to continue their own task (*TT*, IV, viii). Beyond what this moment means for readers, for Sam and Frodo, the "citation" of the Elder Days functions as a reference to a past reality, a history that they both learned and now employ to their own recovery. To think of the First Age materials diegetically, then, privileges their existence for those dwelling in Arda and asks us to consider them as historical, literary, sacred, and archival material for those inhabitants.

Because the War of Wrath that closes the First Age results in catastrophe and cataclysm in the disappearance of Beleriand – the very lands and locales where the Great Tales take place – the preservation of those tales in their various forms becomes the primary way of retaining the memories of the peoples and lands so vital to the remaining peoples of Middle-earth. As John Marino notes, "comparison of the past and present asks for an affective response to what no longer is";[6] for those who

6. Marino, John, "The Presence of the Past in *The Lord of the Rings*", *Tolkien in the New Century; Essays in Honor of Tom Shippey*, ed. by John Houghton, Janet Brennan Croft, Nancy Martsch, John D. Rateliff, and Robin Anne Reid, (McFarland, 2014), p. 181.

survived and for those who come after, the tales of the Elder Days function as the elegiac repository of what no longer is, and characters' various affective responses underline the ways that these moments hallow a past and create meaning in a present.

While my work with the Eldar Days has tended to examine the texts diegetically,[7] the fascinating thing about what Christopher Tolkien has given us is that the First Age materials function continually on both levels, diegetic and non-diegetic. They resonate both as records of Tolkien's sub-creation made and re-made throughout the twentieth century, and as a cache of ancient tales of the Elder Days that preserve and hallow the Great Tales of "the drowned lands" (*CoH*, 8) of Beleriand. In fact, in their discussion and commentary about the First Age, both Tolkien and his son were able to move with great facility back and forth, between discussing how Tolkien created and revised the world known as Arda (non-diegetic discussions) and discussing tales-events-peoples-maps of Arda as if they in fact existed (diegetically). Maureen Mann notes that, according to Arne Zettersten, Tolkien "could dwell in both worlds at the same time or enjoy an interplay between them. These tracks between the two worlds ran very closely together and Tolkien could rush along them simultaneously."[8]

---

7. See Agan, Cami D., "An Account of a Lost Geography: 'Of Beleriand and Its Realms'," *Journal of the Fantastic in the Arts*, 30.1 (2019), 85-102. See also Nagy, Gergely, "The Adapted Text: The Lost Poetry of Beleriand." *Tolkien Studies*, 1.1 (2004), 21-41.

8. Mann, Maureen, "Artefacts and Immersion in the Worldbuilding of Tolkien and the Brontës" *Sub-Creating Arda; World-Building in J.R.R. Tolkien's Work, Its Precursors and Its Legacies*, ed. by Dimitra Fimi and Thomas Honegger (Zurich: Walking Tree, 2019), p. 351. Her reference is to Arne Zettersten, *J.R.R. Tolkien's Double Worlds and Creative Process; Language and Life* (New York: Palgrave, 2011), p.25.

Indeed, both father and son lived the construction of the world, its sub-creation, and within the sphere of Arda – discussing it, amending it, writing letters about it, and then editing, publishing these works – and both were able to write of the non-diegetic and diegetic interplay with ease. For example, Christopher describes the First Age materials as "the old legends ('old' now not only in their derivation from the remote First Age, but also in terms of my father's life) became the vehicle and depository of his profoundest reflections" (*Silmarillion*, 7). By noting that "old legends" accurately describes both their existence in Tolkien's process of writing and in the world of Arda (7), Christopher's reveals his ability to "dwell in both worlds at the same time or enjoy an interplay between them. He reflects on the dual sense of the tales' ancient qualities: they are old diegetically (from the Elder Days) and non-diegetically (they are the earliest his father conceived). His father, likewise, sustained discussions of the Primary and Secondary world value of the First Age legends simultaneously: "They arose in my mind as 'given' things, and as they came, separately, so too the links grew. . . always I had the sense of recording what was already 'there'. Somewhere: not of 'inventing'" (*Silmarillion*, xii). Intriguingly, Tolkien both acknowledges his role in making or sub-creation (a non-diegetic position) and suggests that elements of the world of Arda already "exist" (placing himself in the world of Arda, in the diegesis of that place).

Ideally, as readers, scholars, and fans of Tolkien, we have the chance to expand our abilities to see the Elder Days both non-diegetically and diegetically, to dwell in both worlds. We can appreciate the decades-long process of creation and editing that brought the texts to us in all their dizzying variety, and we can appreciate how those texts also exist for characters within

Middle-earth. We can note the ways the texts hearken to the sub-creator and his cultural context, his writing process, and his interest in common themes, and we can note the ways tales, songs, and objects weave their way from the First Age into the consciousness of later inhabitants of Arda. With father and son as our guides, we can work to attain this fluidity between the diegetic world of Arda, whose inhabitants still celebrate the brave deeds of Beren and Lúthien, and the non-diegetic world of the sub-creator and editor, who have made the created world "real" for us. Thanks to Christopher's First Age publications, we can at least make the attempt to inhabit both worlds.

Bibliography

Agan, Cami D., "An Account of a Lost Geography: 'Of Beleriand and Its Realms'", *Journal of the Fantastic in the Arts*, 30.1 (2019), 85-102.

Drout, Michael, et. al, "Tolkien's Creation of the Impression of Depth", *Tolkien Studies*, 11 (2014), 167-211.

Fisher, Jason, "From Mythopoeia to Mythography: Tolkien, Lonnröt, and Jerome", *The Silmarillion Thirty Years On*," ed. by Allan Turner, (Zurich: Walking Tree, 2007), pp.111-38.

Mann, Maureen, "Artefacts and Immersion in the Worldbuilding of Tolkien and the Brontës", *Sub-Creating Arda; World-Building in J.R.R. Tolkien's Work, Its Precursors and Its Legacies*, ed. by Dimitra Fimi and Thomas Honegger, (Zurich: Walking Tree, 2019), pp. 335-358.

Marino, John, "The Presence of the Past in *The Lord of the Rings*. Tolkien in the New Century' *Essays in Honor of Tom Shippey*. ed. by John Houghton, Janet Brennan Croft, Nancy Martsch, John D. Rateliff, and Robin Anne Reid (Jefferson, NC: McFarland, 2014), pp. 169-81.

Nagy, Gergely, "The Adapted Text: The Lost Poetry of Beleriand", *Tolkien Studies*, 1 (2004), 21-41.

Shippey, T.A., *The Road to Middle-earth: How J.R.R. Tolkien Created a New Mythology*, (Boston: Houghton, 2003).

Tolkien, Christopher, Foreword to *The Book of Lost Tales Part I*, by J.R.R. Tolkien (Boston: Houghton, 1984), pp. 1-11.
—— Preface to *The Children of Húrin* by J.R.R. Tolkien (Boston: Houghton, 2007), pp.7-11.
—— Preface to *The Fall of Gondolin* by J.R.R. Tolkien (Boston: Houghton, 2018), pp.9-19.
—— Introduction to "Ainulindalë." *Morgoth's Ring* by J.R.R. Tolkien (Boston: Houghton, 1993, pp. 3-8.
—— Foreword to *The Peoples of Middle-earth*, by J.R.R. Tolkien (Boston:

Houghton, 1986), pp. vii-xiii.

—— Foreword to *The Silmarillion*, 2nd ed, (Boston: Houghton, 1977), pp. 7-9.

—— Introduction to *Unfinished Tales*, (Boston: Houghton, 1980), pp.1-14.

Tolkien, J.R.R., *The Hobbit*, (Boston: Houghton, 1994).

—— Preface to *The Silmarillion*, ed. by Christopher Tolkien, 2nd ed, (Boston: Houghton, 2001, pp.xi-xxiv.

—— *The Two Towers*, (New York: Ballantine, 1965).

Wolf, Mark J. P., "More than a Story: Narrative Threads and Narrative Fabric," *Building Imaginary Worlds; The Theory and History of Sub-Creation* (New York: Routledge, 2012), pp. 198-225.

Zettersten, Arne, *J.R.R. Tolkien's Double Worlds and Creative Process; Language and Life* (New York: Palgrave, 2011).

The other illustrated *Silmarillion*: Francis Mosley for the Folio Society[1]

Marie Bretagnolle

There were many adaptations of J.R.R. Tolkien's works in the form of illustrated editions in the 1990s. In 1998, no less than two books were published with original illustrations: David Wyatt's Hobbit and Ted Nasmith's *Silmarillion*. Nasmith's well-known and well-loved version was released shortly after another illustrated Silmarillion, by Francis Mosley for the Folio Society. Francis Mosley had already worked several times for this publishing house, but he was given a rather unusual task with this commission, the roots of which go back to the 1970s when the Folio Society published *The Lord of the Rings* and *The Hobbit*.

This paper will shed light on Mosley's lesser-known illustrated *Silmarillion* and how it was conceived. To do so, I had the pleasure of getting in touch with the artist himself who agreed to answer some of my questions. I would like to thank Francis Mosley for his time and for allowing me to show his illustrations in my paper.

---

1. A translation of this paper in French is available on my PhD blog here: https://voirtolkien.hypotheses.org/633.

1. How the edition came to be

1.1. J.R.R. Tolkien and the Folio Society

In 1977, the Folio Society published an illustrated edition of *The Lord of the Rings*. It was illustrated by the Princess Margrethe of Denmark, under the pseudonym of Ingahild Grathmer, and by Eric Fraser, a British illustrator. The Princess and Tolkien had exchanged letters and she had enclosed some sketches that the Professor appreciated. These sketches were redrawn by Fraser to become the illustrations for the 1977 edition of *The Lord of the Rings*. In 1979, Fraser alone illustrated *The Hobbit* for the same publishing house. He took care to keep a similar style in his pictures so that the books would form a whole. Twenty years later, the Folio Society wished to publish an illustrated *Silmarillion*, but sadly Eric Fraser had passed away in 1983. The publishers turned to Francis Mosley, who had worked with them since the early 1980s, illustrating for instance novels by Sir Arthur Conan Doyle.

The set of Tolkien books by the Folio Society had to have a visual unity. This implied an identical repartition of the illustrations within the pages, with a full-page frontispiece illustration and smaller, landscape-format chapter headings, but it also meant for Mosley to create pictures in the style of another artist, or rather, two other artists.

1.2 Mosley's style

Mosley describes his own style as: "a quite traditional pen and ink cross hatched style in the tradition of Tenniel (*Alice in Wonderland*) and a lot of the Punch illustrators of the late nineteenth century"[2] He works in gradients of grey rather than solid black and white.

He usually draws on a surface twice the size of the finished picture. This is a common illustration trick which enables the artist to be more precise and detailed than in a smaller piece. For *The Silmarillion*, he started with pencil sketches, then traced over with pen. The black areas were painted in gouache, and he added details in white. Gouache is a very opaque, water-based medium which lends itself quite well to contrasted pieces in black-and-white. It enabled Mosley to imitate Fraser's distinctive style which he describes as "more wood-engraving-like, more patterned". And indeed, Fraser favoured areas of solid black contrasting with a white background.

1.3 A harmonised corpus

Mosley considered this an interesting challenge and enjoyed exploring a completely different style, with the reassurance that the pictures that started it all, the Princess's drawings, had been enjoyed by Tolkien himself. There was a voluntary continuity. Mosley studied Fraser's illustrations and copied some features, such as "the scales on Eric Fraser's dragons". He paid attention to the small details that would make his pictures echo those of his predecessor. In chapter 20 (*Silmarillion*, 221, see fig. 1), he copied Smaug's anatomy from the chapter "Inside Information" (*Hobbit*, 172) to depict another dragon. This illustration is inspired by the following lines:

---

2. All of Mosley's quotes are taken from our personal correspondence.

But even as the vanguard of Maedhros came upon the Orcs, Morgoth loosed his last strength, and Angband was emptied. There came wolves, and wolfriders, and there came Balrogs, and dragons, and Glaurung father of dragons. The strength and terror of the Great Worm were now great indeed [...] (*Silmarillion*, 226-227).[3]

Mosley's dragon is pictured in three-quarters, launching himself into battle, amidst the army of Morgoth. His great black wings stand out against the white walls of Angband. The only dragon described in detail in the book is Glaurung. In the next chapter, "Of Túrin Turambar", he is shown as a "coiling" (*Silmarillion*, 252) "Great Worm" (*Silmarillion*, 260), with "serpent-eyes" (*Silmarillion*, 251). Mosley was well aware of Glaurung's characteristics, and chose to stay faithful to Fraser's archetype by illustrating another dragon from the host of Morgoth. He explains:

[...] any dragon I drew followed [Fraser's] original conception of Smaug. [...] Chapter headings play a different role to illustrations embodied in the text they are not trying to show what happened but to set the mood. The dragon shown was not a depiction of Glaurung who was wingless.

In chapter 20, Mosley did not take the most expected path. He chose to illustrate the impression of fear surrounding the dragon, in order to make sure his book tied in with Fraser's pictures in previous editions. This meant that he moved a little away from the text in this one case.

---

3. Page numbers refer to the Folio Society edition of the text.

2. Creating the illustrations

2.1. Interlacing images

Within the book, another degree of unity is achieved by reusing motifs from one illustration to another. For instance, vaulted ceilings appear in three different locations: Aulë's underground halls in chapter 2 (*Silmarillion,* 47), the "fastness of Mandos" (*Silmarillion,* 58) in chapter 6 (*Silmarillion,* 71, see fig. 2) and Menegroth in chapter 10 (*Silmarillion,* 105).

By limiting the visual overload that a book like *The Silmarillion* can inspire, the artist leaves room for the readers' imagination. This was essential for Tolkien. In footnote E of "On Fairy-stories", he declared that illustrations did not serve a fantasy text in that they put forth one interpretation and prevented the readers from creating their own mental images. Mosley's pictures, like Fraser and Princess Margrethe's before, counter this argument by a stylisation of shapes that does not pin down exactly what something or someone looks like. This enables the artist to repeat the motif of the vaulted ceiling without making the reader feel like all scenes take place in the same location, because he introduces variations in each illustration. Whether this is a conscious decision on Mosley's part or not, his choice of subjects to depict creates a unity within the book.

2.2 Reading the text as an illustrator

This choice could be a question of taste, if an artist enjoys a particular scene, but more often the criteria are slightly different. Here is a point on which Francis Mosley and Ted

Nasmith, who have worked on the same text, follow opposite directions. Nasmith likes to illustrate moments of tension, when dramatic action is taking place, whether this concerns characters, as in "The Kinslaying at Alqualondë" (*Silmarillion,* 1998, 78), or the whole invented world, as in "The First Dawn of the Sun" (*Silmarillion,* 1998, 92).

Mosley usually stayed away from those moments and looked for passages with "interesting imagery", in his own words. Only a third of his illustrations (9 out of 29) depict characters, and most of them are very stylized, or seen from afar. Most of the time, he chose more abstract subjects, for instance in chapter 4, "Of Thingol and Melian" (*Silmarillion,* 63, see fig. 3). This very short chapter describes Melian's songs and her meeting with Elwë, who later becomes known as Thingol. To illustrate it, Mosley used the visual metaphor of the bird, for Melian, and the motif of the tree. The latter is self-explanatory and represents both the forest where Melian dwelt and the one where she came to live with Thingol, in Doriath. The artist combined the two elements in his picture. He kept the shapes quite simple, with almost no sense of perspective except the fact that the trees in the background are smaller than the birds in the foreground. The symmetry enhances the overall symbolism of the piece which manages to evoke the contents of the chapter without actually spoiling any of it for the reader.

2.3 Illustrating the text for readers

According to Mosley, illustrations should neither distract from the text nor contradict it, but they should echo, expand or play with the story:

There is a balance to be struck between the image in the writing that is visually most appealing and yet avoiding choosing the most dramatic events where there is a risk that your interpretation could come into conflict with the reader's imagination. [In] Chapter 10 Tolkien gives a precise description: "The pillars of Menegroth were hewn in the likeness of [the] beeches [of Oromë]" [(*Silmarillion*, 108)] so here this image appealed and I gave it form. What you hope is that the pictures complement the writing, not that they create a story but perhaps allow you to look around within the story that has been written.

Mosley often used symbolism in his illustrations to detach them from the narration while still inscribing them in the world of Middle-earth. It is also a way for the pictures to reach beyond the limited space devoted to them at the beginning of each chapter.

In Chapter 1 of the "Quenta Silmarillion", "Of the Beginning of Days" (*Silmarillion*, 37, see fig. 4), Mosley represented the Two Trees of Valinor. In the story, these sacred trees indicate time through their waxing and waning. Mosley did not make clear which one was Telperion, the silver tree, and which one was Laurelin, the golden one. In that regard, the artist illustrates a specific passage of the text, when Tolkien describes the "gentle hour of softer light when both trees were faint and their gold and silver beams were mingled" (*Silmarillion*, 41). Mosley even depicted the beams of light issuing from them. And yet, his picture is open to interpretation since there is no colour to differentiate the two trees. Mosley does not repeat what the text already says, but offers a symbolic representation of the trees.

3. Mosley's artistic choices

3.1. Historical influences

Even though he had a design brief, in that he had to create pictures in a specific style, the commission left him with a certain amount of creative freedom. Most of the locations, people and artefacts in the book were unheard of in *The Lord of the Rings* or in *The Hobbit*, so he could not always take inspiration from Fraser and Princess Margrethe as he had done with dragons.

Knowing the writer's field of study, Mosley turned to the Anglo-Saxon period in several of his illustrations. The most striking example is chapter 21, "Of Túrin Turambar" (*Silmarillion*, 233, see fig. 5). This picture will feel familiar to people who share Tolkien's interests since it is largely inspired by the Anglo-Saxon helmet discovered at Sutton Hoo in 1939[4]. Tolkien did not describe Túrin's helmets precisely in the text. One is referred to as "the Dragon-helm of Dor-lómin" (*Silmarillion*, 234), but it is not Túrin's only helmet. Later in the text is mentioned "a Dwarf-mask all gilded" (*Silmarillion*, 247). The motif of the helm permeates the chapter in additional ways. Túrin names himself "Gorthol, the Dread Helm" (*Silmarillion*, 242), and the different names he takes move the story forward. Identity is a strong theme in this tale, being alternately hidden and revealed, and Mosley enhanced this by picturing an impressive helmet hiding the features of the character wearing it.

4.https://www.britishmuseum.org/collection/death-and-memory/anglo-saxon-ship-burial-sutton-hoo

A simple juxtaposition of the illustration with a photograph of the Sutton Hoo helmet reveals the deep influence of the latter on the former. Mosley adapted several features from the lower half of the helmet, including the fact that most of the face is hidden by decorative plates. He also highlighted the very name of this piece of armour as the "Dragon-helm". To do so, Mosley took the silhouette of a flying beast on the Sutton Hoo helmet, with its wings as the helmet's eyebrows and tail as moustache. He made it even more visible by having the dragon's face protruding from the crown of the helmet and its wings extending on either side. This particular illustration blends seamlessly historical influences and Tolkien's own motifs.

The helmets are not described in details in the text, but it is worth noting when Tolkien wrote the story of *The Children of Húrin*. According to Christopher Tolkien, his father worked on a poem version until 1924-25 (*CoH,* 269-272). He then devoted himself to other stories that would form the future "Silmarillion" until 1937, when he turned to *The Hobbit* and, later, to *The Lord of the Rings*. He only came back to the earlier history of Middle-earth from 1950 onwards. At this date the Sutton Hoo grave had been unearthed in Suffolk and Tolkien was most probably aware of the discoveries, but I do not think anyone has found evidence that he was inspired by the findings.

3.2. Showing and hiding

Choosing to depict this anonymous helmet in the chapter heading shows how Mosley considers the placement of the pictures within the book and how they interact with the text. Some illustrators take great cares to depict the passages closest to where the illustrations are put in a book. Alan Lee, for instance, does not want the reader to leaf through the volume searching for a correspondence between the image and the text. This often leads him to illustrate passages of lesser dramatic intensity because he cannot choose where the pictures appear. Ted Nasmith was also careful to place text and image close to each other in his 1998 illustrated *Silmarillion*. However, he was free to place the images where he wanted because the book was printed on a glossy paper which supports both text and image, so he could choose the subjects he most wanted to paint.

Mosley, on the reverse, is not necessarily looking for such closeness, because the place devoted to the images is fixed: with the only exception of the frontispiece, they are set above each chapter title. In some instances, Mosley chooses to illustrate exclusively the first lines of the section. In other chapters, he anticipates on the text. On those occasions, his symbolic style prevents the reader from being spoilt too much of the story. When chapter 19 "Of Beren and Lúthien" (*Silmarillion*, 190, see fig. 6) opens, there is no telling who the two animals are. The readers will discover what the illustration is about only after reading the corresponding passage in the chapter. In this case, the interpretation is rather straightforward, but it is not always so.

In chapter 6 "Of Fëanor and the Unchaining of Melkor" (*Silmarillion*, 71), the readers are free to interpret the illustration in different ways. It could either depict Melkor being kept prisoner, buried under coils of chains, or it might just as well represent his unchaining since the character is not visible. Mosley plays with showing and hiding to keep the reader in doubt and not reveal too much, since the title of the chapter already tells quite a lot about its contents.

In such illustrations, the artist leaves interpretation to the readers, making them take part in the relation between text and image. Without being aware of it, he complied to Christopher Tolkien's wishes. Working with Alan Lee, Christopher Tolkien asked him explicitly not to depict Melkor in *Beren and Lúthien*[5]. By avoiding the representation of characters, Mosley came to the same conclusion and used visual metaphors in many cases.

Conclusion

The Folio Society undertook to publish an illustrated *Silmarillion* in a decade when many new illustrated Tolkien books appeared. They paid attention to the author's opinion on illustrations in order to create a book in which image and text worked hand-in-hand. To do so, Mosley found a balance between dramatic moments, often seen from an unexpected angle so that the characters are in fact out-of-frame, and more evocative pictures, in which he suggested Tolkien's intricate world-building and created visual links from one illustration to another. To him, "the image is less about story telling (not least because that is already in the text) but adding an atmosphere that is complementary to the writing". He conveyed this atmosphere by focusing on landscape and key material elements from the story rather than characters or actions.

For Francis Mosley, this meant an exercise in artistic flexibility as he studied another artist's style and made it his own by exploring new subjects and landscapes. Appropriating

---

5. Alan Lee explained this in the interview I conducted for the French national Library on 6 February 2020. The interview was filmed and is available here: https://youtu.be/Wkzyfp0hmys (at the 32:40 mark). For a full transcript in English, see my blog post here: https://voirtolkien.hypotheses.org/584.

Fraser's graphic, black-and-white style was a challenge that he enjoyed, motivated as he was by the idea that Tolkien approved the pictures the artist took inspiration from. With this edition, the Folio Society and Francis Mosley sought to answer the thorny question of what kind of pictures the author would have liked, with the added difficulty that this particular book was not published in his lifetime.

Bibliography

McIlwaine, Catherine, *Tolkien: Maker of Middle-Earth* (Oxford: Bodleian Library, 2018).

Tolkien, J.R.R., Ingahild Grathmer, and Eric Fraser, *The Lord of the Rings* (London: Folio Society, 1977).

Tolkien, J.R.R., and Eric Fraser, *The Hobbit* (London: Folio Society, 1979).

Tolkien, J.R.R., *The Monsters and the Critics and Other Essays*, ed. by Christopher Tolkien (London: George Allen and Unwin, 1983).

Hammond, Wayne G. and Christina Scull, *J.R.R. Tolkien: artist & illustrator* (Boston: Houghton Mifflin, 1995).

Tolkien, J.R.R., and Francis Mosley, *The Silmarillion*, ed. by Christopher Tolkien (London: Folio Society, 1997).

Tolkien, J.R.R., and Ted Nasmith, *The Silmarillion*, ed. by Christopher Tolkien (London: HarperCollins, 1998).

Tolkien, J.R.R., and Ted Nasmith, *The Silmarillion*, ed. by Christopher Tolkien (London: HarperCollins, 2004).

Fig. 1. Francis Mosley, *Of the Fifth Battle: Nirnaeth Arnoediad*, gouache. Illustration for chapter 20 of *The Silmarillion* (London: Folio Society, 1997).

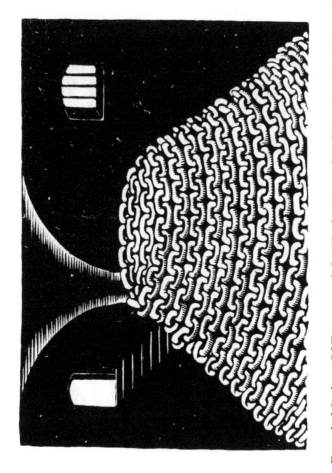

Fig. 2. Francis Mosley, *Of Fëanor and the Unchaining of Melkor*, gouache. Illustration for chapter 6 of *The Silmarillion* (London: Folio Society, 1997).

Fig. 3. Francis Mosley, *Of Thingol and Melian*, gouache. Illustration for chapter 4 of *The Silmarillion* (London: Folio Society, 1997).

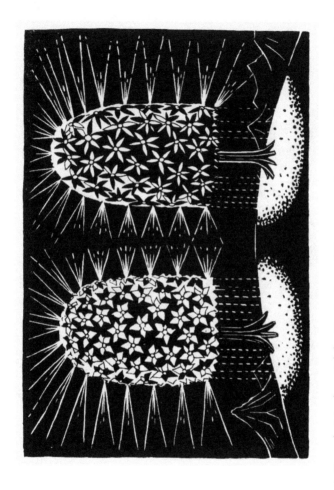

Fig. 4. Francis Mosley, *Of the Beginning of Days*, gouache. Illustration for chapter 1 of *The Silmarillion* (London: Folio Society, 1997).

Fig. 5. Francis Mosley, *Of Túrin Turambar*, gouache. Illustration for chapter 21 of *The Silmarillion* (London: Folio Society, 1997).

Fig. 6. Francis Mosley, *Of Beren and Lúthien*, gouache. Illustration for chapter 19 of *The Silmarillion* (London: Folio Society, 1997).

Elvish as She is Filmed:
The Adaption of the Elvish Language in Peter Jackson's *The Lord of the Rings*

Dr. Andrew Higgins

During the lockdown period due to the corona-virus pandemic the cast and artistic team of Peter Jackson's film adaptation of J.R.R. Tolkien's *The Lord of the Rings* (first released in cinemas from 2001-2003) were re-united through the magic of the Zoom digital platform as part of an effort to raise money for health charities. In the course of the cast's conversations and reminiscing Liv Tyler, who played Arwen Undómiel in the films, astounded her fellow cast members by reciting from memory the Elvish phrase which in the film she had hurled at the Black Riders at the Fords of Bruinen after the now famous line, 'if you want him, come and claim him'.[1] After over 20 years, Liv Tyler was still able to intone the Elvish incantation that temporarily stopped the Black Riders from their pursuit of the One Ring.

> Nîn o Chithaeglir
> lasto beth daer;
> Rimmo nîn Bruinen
> dan in Ulaer![2]

---

1. *The Fellowship of the Ring*, dir. by Peter Jackson (New Line Cinema, 2001). 17th Scene (21st in Extended Edition)
2. Ibid.

In Tolkien's original text we only learn later in Rivendell that it is was Elrond who commanded the flood. Gandalf tells Frodo, 'the river of this valley is under his power, and it will rise in anger when he has great need to bar the Ford' (*FR*, II, i). In this cinematic adaptation not only is the instrument of the flood changed but the new summoner of the flood – Arwen – is given words to command the waters of the mountain. The spell in the film is made up of a series of attested words from Tolkien's invented language of Sindarin, one of the two major languages of the Elves in Middle-earth. A review of these attested words, or elements of the words that appear in the corpus of Tolkien's known Sindarin language invention render this passage in English as follows:

Oh Waters of the Misty Mountains
listen to my great word;
flow you waters of the Loudwater
against the Ringwraiths![3]

While all these Sindarin words can in some form be found in various versions of Tolkien's corpus of language invention inextricably linked to his myth-making and world-building, the entirety of the spell itself is clearly not Tolkien's. What this passage signifies was a desire from the earliest pre-planning for *The Lord of the Rings* films by the team of Peter Jackson, Fran Walsh and Philippa Boyens to use the languages of Middle-earth as one of the key world-building elements in their adapted version of Tolkien's mythopoeia. The motivation for this came especially from a desire Peter Jackson had to not

3. Based on the author's own translation.

make a 'standard' fantasy film. In an interview, Jackson said that Tolkien writes in a way that makes everything come alive, and we wanted to set that realistic feeling of an ancient world come to life right away with the first film, then continue to build it as the story unravels.[4]

Producer and co-writer Philippa Boyens (who of the three members of the creative team had the most familiarity and passion for Tolkien's works going into the process) said that she wanted to create a depth in the film narrative, 'that would elevate their films above the gaudy clichés of the barbarian hordes'.[5] Thus, very much like Tolkien, the filmmakers wanted to create a cinematic world that had historic depth and, as Tolkien himself said of his invented languages, 'an illusion of historicity' (*Letters*, 143). Clearly, one of the key objectives towards achieving this was through the deliberate use of elements of Tolkien's languages in the films. Indeed the first words we hear in *The Fellowship of the Ring* are in an adapted form of Elvish. The importance of this opening dialogue being in Elvish is underscored by the fact that originally this passage was delivered in English by Cate Blanchett the actress who plays Galadriel. According to Philippa Boyens it was only later at the post-production A.D.R. (Automated Digital Replacement) recording session that co-writer and producer Fran Walsh asked if they could overlay this opening English passage with Elvish, 'we want the sense of the strangeness of the history' Walsh commented.[6] Therefore, the adapters used a passage which in the novel was originally spoken in English

4. Ian Nathan, *Anything You Can Imagine Peter Jackson and the Making of Middle-earth* (London: HarperCollins, 2018), p. 15.

5. Nathan, p.16.

6. Nathan, p. 22.

by Treebeard (*RK*, II, vi) but now would be intoned by Cate Blanchett/Galadriel first in Elvish and then in English with the lines '*I amar prestar aen, han mathon ne nen, han mathon ne chae a han noston ned 'wilith* – the world is changed; I can feel it in the water; I can feel it in the earth, I can smell it in the air'.[7]

This bilingual opening passage introduces the history of the forging of the rings and plunges the viewer directly into the historical depth and strangeness of Middle-earth. There is an interesting parallel here with Tolkien's own first use of Elvish in *The Lord of the Rings* during the Hobbits' encounter with Gildor Inglorion. Through the use of Elvish Tolkien introduces the reader to an older world than the Shire and creates the sense of strangeness as the Hobbits journey deeper and deeper into Faërie.[8] In this adaptation it is the viewer who, through the use of Elvish in the first lines of the movie, is immediately plunged into Jackson's version of cinematic Faërie.

For the balance of this paper I want to explore how this version of Elvish was actually constructed and focus in on several examples of diegetic Elvish dialogue to suggest that the inclusion of Elvish in the films creates for those with some awareness or knowledge of Tolkien's languages a sense of familiarity while for others a sense of strangeness and depth of history in Jackson's cinematic Faërie.

To start with Tolkien's own languages, in his seminal work

---

7. *The Fellowship of the Ring*, dir. by Peter Jackson (New Line Cinema, 2001). 1st Scene.

8. Explored further by the author in Andrew Higgins, 'Mythology is Language and Language is Mythology How Verlyn Flieger's Favourite Bumper-sticker works in Tolkien's Legendarium' in *A Wilderness of Dragons Essays in Honour of Verlyn Flieger,* ed. John D. Rateliff (Minnesota: The Gabro Head, 2018), pp. 105-107.

'Elvish as She is Spoke' scholar and editor of Tolkien's language papers Carl F. Hostetter has noted that Tolkien's overall objective in inventing his languages was not to create a homogenous series of languages that could be used for conversation and dialogue.[9] Tolkien's Elvish language invention which started in his pre-World War One notebooks resulted in several different versions of Elvish created over different creative periods. The nature of Tolkien's language invention is best summed up in his own words in an unsent draft of a response letter to a Mr. Rang, 'it must be emphasised that this process of invention was/is a private enterprise undertaken to give pleasure to myself by giving expression to my personal linguistic 'aesthetic' or taste and its fluctuations.' (*Letters*, 380) Hostetter characterises the body and make-up of Tolkien's known language invention as 'a sequence of more-or-less complete and more-or-less variant and even conflicting versions of historical grammars, almost always heavily weighted toward the phonology, describing versions of his invented languages as they were conceived at various points in his lifetime.'[10]

When it came to carrying out the plan to include elements of Tolkien's languages in the dialogue for the films, the adapter would face a rather daunting task of working with a body of language invention that was neither consistent nor complete and invented by a man who when interviewed said he would not mind people knowing and enjoying Elvish but not have people speaking it. As Tolkien said when he was interviewed in the *Tolkien in Oxford* documentary, 'No I don't desire to have

9. This seminal work of Tolkien linguistic scholarship can be found here https://www.elvish.org/articles/EASIS.pdf (last accessed 22/08/2020).
10. Carl F. Hostetter 'Elvish as She is Spoke' https://www.elvish.org/articles/EASIS.pdf, p. 238.

an afternoon talking to chaps one thing of course is Elvish is too complicated I never finished making it'.[11] Of course, given Hostetter's characterisation above, the adapter of Tolkien's languages for the films would have a bit more to work with than the more recent adapter of George R.R. Martin's invented languages of Dothraki and High Valyrian from the *Song of Ice and Fire* texts for HBO's *Game of Thrones* series. In this case Martin had only invented about 50 words of Dothraki and a few phrases of High Valyrian which the language inventor for the series, linguist David J. Peterson, successfully crafted into languages that could be used for extensive dialogue and became so extensive that there are currently courses being offered on the language app Duolingo to learn them.[12]

The work of inventing these passages of Elvish and the other examples of dialogue in various forms of Tolkien's languages fell to another linguist, David Salo, who read Tolkien's works when he was a boy and was fascinated by the languages. In interviews he cites Tolkien's notes in the song cycle book *The Road Goes Ever On* to the *Namarië* and *Elbereth* poems as especially helpful in learning elements of the Elvish languages.[13] Salo went on to study Latin, Greek and linguistics at Macalester College in Minnesota. In 1998 he was one of the founders of the Elfing mail list for Tolkien language enthusiasts. Based on interviews he has

---

11. Stuart D. Lee 'Tolkien in Oxford (BBC, 1968) A Reconstruction' in *Tolkien Studies* vol 15 (Western Virginia University Press, 2018), pp.152-153.
12. The process Peterson followed is fully explored in David J. Peterson *The Art of Language Invention: From Horse Lords to Dark Elves the Words Behind World-Building.* (New York, Penguin Books, 2015).
13. J.R.R. Tolkien and Donald Swan *The Road Goes Ever On A Song Cycle.* (London: HarperCollins, 2002), pp. 60-65.

given Salo seems to have become involved with the preparation for the movies when he heard they were in pre-production.[14] He contacted one of the films artists and designers, John Howe, and offered his services and knowledge of Tolkien's languages. Howe asked him to design an inscription for Bilbo's sword Sting in Elvish expressed in the Elvish writing script of tengwar. Salo came up with the inscription 'They Call me Sharp-point I am the Slayer of Spiders'. Howe then recommended Salo to Philippa Boyens to work on all the dialogue in the film that adapted Tolkien's languages as well as inscriptions in both tengwar and Cirth for the props and documents, manuscripts seen in the films and the Elvish lyrics for the movie soundtracks by Howard Shore (and later Salo would do the same for the three *Hobbit* movies). Salo did all of this via email from his home in Wisconsin (he never visited the filming locations in New Zealand) and would make recordings of the dialogue which would be sent to the team in New Zealand for the dialogue coaches to work with the actors on.

The actual process of adaptation involved Salo being sent short passages of dialogue from the writers to translate. Salo has stated that he never saw the whole shooting script and was only sent passages in batches. In describing the process he followed, Salo shows indications that he understood the fluctuating nature of the languages Tolkien invented and the fact that the languages for the most part were not intended to be used for standard dialogue.[15] Salo arrived at the translation

14. Salo discusses how he became involved with the films in this online interview here https://www.youtube.com/watch?v=SG5MycI-SOs and see also http://tolkiengateway.net/wiki/David_Salo last accessed 20/08/2020).
15. Cited from http://newboards.theonering.net/forum/gforum/perl/gforum. cgi?post=390356 (last accessed 20/08/2020).

of English into Elvish dialogue by doing three things:

1)   Identify the key words in the sentence
2)   Rearrange them into a different order that would correspond to the structures of the Elvish (based on his understanding of Tolkien's languages)
3)   'Translate' the individual words

When it came to step three, Salo would be faced with a series of options. Either the actual words already existed in the corpus of Tolkien's language invention which Salo could use. However, what if the word did not exist in Tolkien's corpus? The process Salo said he would use to construct an Elvish word is quite interesting. In one interview Salo said, 'He (Tolkien) gives little hints here and there. So you look at that, you look at the patterns, and you extrapolate'.[16] In constructing a non-Tolkien attested Elvish word Salo said he would start by going 'to the known roots and structures of the languages'.[17] For a word in Sindarin, Salo often looked at attested words in Quenya to see if there was a possible cognate. Like real-world languages Quenya and Sindarin have a mutual ancestor in Common Eldarin. For real languages that share a common ancestor, linguists can trace back from more recent forms that share a common ancestor, linguists can trace back from the more recent forms to reconstruct the original ones. Therefore, in constructing new Elvish words Salo was using the established structure that Tolkien created for the (feigned) historical development of his languages

---

16. Cited from http://www.theonering.net/torwp/2011/09/11/47992-david-salo-linguistic-consultant-for-the-hobbit-speaks-at-geek-kon/ (last accessed 21/08/2020).
17. Ibid.

using the similar reconstructive methods of the 19th century philologists which in Tolkien inspired such constructs as his 'Tree of Tongues' based on August Schleicher's *Stammbaum* or developmental tree of language.[18]

When it came to inventing the Elvish words that did not exist Salo had to dip deeply into Tolkien's soup of language invention and employ some Elven skill of his own to twist the language to his needs. In this respect what Salo invented was one strand of a related body of language invention that has come to be called Neo-Elvish – it is Elvish but not the Elvish of Tolkien.[19] One of the key texts that have come from this practice is Salo's own *A Gateway to Sindarin* (2004) which summarises much of the reconstructive (or possibly invention) work Salo did on the films and offers its readers a historical analysis of the Sindarin language and whose reconstructive techniques has caused much discussion and debate in the Tolkien language community.[20]

In 'Elvish as She is Spoke' Hostetter outlines two key methodologies Salo and other practitioners of Neo-Elvish use to work with the body of Tolkien's existing and known language invention and which is prevalent in the Elvish dialogue in films. The first of these is *conflation* which is the homogenising and standardising of language materials from different phases of

18. J.R.R. Tolkien, 'Tengwesta Qenderinwa and Pre-Fëanorian Alphabets' in *Parma Eldalamberon* XVIII (edited by Christopher Gilson, Arden R Smith and Patrick H. Wynne), pp. 28-9, 81.
19. See here for a good overview of Neo-Elvish http://tolkiengateway.net/wiki/Neo-Elvish (last accessed 22/08/2020).
20. A good and balanced summary of the critical reception of Salo's *A Gateway to Sindarin* can be found here: http://tolkiengateway.net/wiki/A_Gateway_to_Sindarin#Critical_reception (last accessed 23/08/2020).

Tolkien's language invention. In a sense this suggests that the dialogue being spoken by the Elves in the movies consists of many historical different versions of Elvish. It would be as if we spoke in an English that had some Old English, Middle English and Modern English in one line of dialogue. A good example of this in Elvish dialogue in the films is Salo's invention of a Sindarin word 'boe' to create the obligatory phrase 'we need/ it is necessary'. This construction is found in this dialogue by Aragorn to Haldir in Lórien.

Haldir o Lórien.
Henio, aníron, boe ammen i dulu lîn.
Boe ammen veriad lîn.[21]

To construct, or translate, this English word into Elvish, Salo went to Tolkien's 1938 *Etymologies* and found Tolkien's proto-Eldarin root MBAW which formed words having to do with 'compel, force, subject, oppress' (*Lost Road*, 372).[22] The entry also listed the Noldorin (not Sindarin) word reconstructed *bui which signified need. Salo would include this conflation in his 2004 text *A Gateway to Sindarin* as 'Boe Impers. it is necessary, one must, one is compelled to [OS *mbaura < CE *mbauja Root MBAW]'.[23] Noldorin was a form of Elvish

21. *The Fellowship of the Ring*, dir. by Peter Jackson (New Line Cinema, 2001). 31st scene in cinematic edition and 37th in extended edition. The subtitles give the following translation - Haldir from Lórien. 'Understand, I wish [i.e. please, understand!], we need you support [lit. it is necessary to us your help].' 'We need your protection' [Lit. 'it is needed to us your protection'].
22. From which the word Bauglir 'tyrant' as in Morgoth Bauglir derives from.
23. David Salo A Gateway to Sindarin (Utah, Utah University Press, 2004), p. 242.

invented by Tolkien in the late 1920s and 1930s as the next chronological progression from his earliest Elvish language for the exiled Noldoli of Gnomish or Goldogrin which he started inventing in 1917 (*Secret Vice*, xix-xxii). Noldorin features heavily in the *Etymologies* but it surely would not have been the Elvish language that Aragorn would have spoken to Haldir especially as the rest of the dialogue is in the Sindarin of the Third Age of Middle-earth. So again it is a solution to finding a word not attested in Tolkien's language invention but, however close, it conflates two different conceptual periods of Tolkien's language invention into one sentence.

The second method is *reconstruction* which is accomplished by comparing two related languages and through rewinding their respective systems of sound-change recovers forms that must once have been in the shared parent language. An example of this in the films is found in *The Two Towers* in the dialogue at Helm's Deep between Legolas and Aragorn when Legolas says (again using the Noldorin reconstructed boe) 'Boe a hyn neled herain dan caer menig'.[24] Salo indicated that he constructed the Sindarin word for hundred 'herian' from the Quenya word 'haranyë' which actually means the last year of a century in the calendar of Númenor (*RK*, Appendix D, I).

At the beginning of this paper I stated that the cinematic adaptation of Tolkien's Elvish creates a sense of depth and strangeness and clearly it does. However, according to several comments Salo has made in interviews it seems he specifically had some another intentions for the use of Elvish in the films.

---

24. *The Two Towers*, directed by Peter Jackson (New Line Cinema, 2002). 26th scene in cinematic version and thirty-fifth scene in extended edition. The subtitles translate this as 'And they should be three hundred against ten thousand.'

In a revealing posting to the Elfing mail list Salo stated that part of his intention, his particular vision and contribution to this movie, was to create sentences which would be intelligible to the people who study the languages.[25]

Therefore in addition to creating a sense of strangeness, the Elvish languages, as part of Peter Jackson's cinematic Faërie, for the knowing viewer, was also a special series of linguistic 'easter eggs', if you will, containing echoes of words and phrases that would have been familiar from reading the books and studying Tolkien's para-textual language materials to varying degrees. Moreover, there is also the sound-sense of the Elvish language which the dialogue in the films communicates. Salo said that the Sindarin spoken in the film is 'an approximation of how Elf speech might have sounded'.[26] He also commented that he thought the movies were a completely appropriate place for people to encounter the sound and feel of Tolkien's languages.[27] This is especially evident in those scenes in the movies where we hear Elvish dialogue but there are not subtitles given – as in Arwen's spell at The Ford of Bruinen explored above or her command to her horse in the Flight to the Ford – 'noro lim, noro lim, Asfaloth' which comes directly from the novel spoken by Glorfindel and not translated by Tolkien either (*FR*, I, xii). By using the building blocks of Tolkien's Elvish language with its inherent sound-system and

25. Cited from http://tolkiengateway.net/wiki/David_Salo (last accessed 22/08/2020).

26. Cited from http://tolkiengateway.net/wiki/David_Salo (last accessed 22/08/2020).

27. Cited from http://www.theonering.net/torwp/2011/09/11/47992-david-salo-linguistic-consultant-for-the-hobbit-speaks-at-geek-kon/ (last accessed 21/08/2020).

phono-aesthetic natures, not matter how faulty the construction may have been, Salo's adaptation does succeed in creating the sound-sense of the Elvish languages.

In the same interview where Salo thought the movies were a good place for people to encounter the sound and feel of Tolkien's languages he also said, 'I hope that those people who like it [the languages] will move on to the books and try to learn more about them, and about language and linguistics (and life) in general'.[28] This suggests that Salo very much wanted the Elvish, and the other adapted forms of Tolkien's languages, in the films to be gateways for the curious to explore more of not just Tolkien's languages but language in general. Much like many of the first readers of *The Lord of the Rings* sought to learn more about those first phrases they encountered in the novels and the nuggets of linguistic information Tolkien gave in the appendices.

Therefore, while the Elvish language in Peter Jackson and companies' very successful and popular cinematic adaptation of Tolkien's *The Lord of the Rings* is clearly not the Elvish Tolkien would have recognised, it does represent, as a microcosm, the process of adaptation from one medium to another. In this case repurposing a body of disconnected and unfinished language invention to create diegetic dialogue that would suggest the 'sound and feel' of Tolkien's Elvish and the noble race who spoke it. As this paper has shown while there are certainly questions about this adaptation from the Tolkien linguistic point of view, they are far outweighed by hearing Tolkien's languages spoken in Jackson's cinematic world-building and

---

28. Cited from http://www.theonering.net/torwp/2011/09/11/47992-david-salo-linguistic-consultant-for-the-hobbit-speaks-at-geek-kon/ (last accessed 21/08/2020).

Faërie of Middle-earth and if just one (and I am sure there were more) of the audience members new to Tolkien's world left the cinema wanting to learn more about Tolkien's languages, or even language in general, then this work of adaptation was well worth it.

Bibliography

Higgins, Andrew, 'Mythology is Language and Language is Mythology How Verlyn Flieger's Favourite Bumper-sticker works in Tolkien's Legendarium' in *A Wilderness of Dragons Essays in Honour of Verlyn Flieger* ed. by John D. Rateliff (Minnesota: The Gabro Head, 2018).

Hostetter, Carl F., 'Elvish as She is Spoke' (2006) https://www.elvish.org/articles/EASIS.pdf (accessed 24 August 2020).

Lee, Stuart D., 'Tolkien in Oxford (BBC, 1968) A Reconstruction', in *Tolkien Studies* 15 (2018) pp. 115-176.

Nathan, Ian, *Anything You Can Imagine Peter Jackson and the Making of Middle-earth*. (London: HarperCollins, 2018).

Peterson, David J., *The Art of Language Invention: From Horse Lords to Dark Elves the Words Behind World-Building*. (New York, Penguin Books, 2015).

Salo, David, *A Gateway to Sindarin* (Utah, Utah University Press, 2004).

Tolkien, J.R.R., *The Letters of J.R.R. Tolkien*, ed. by Humphrey Carpenter with the assistance of Christopher Tolkien (London: George Allen & Unwin, 1981; Boston: Houghton Mifflin, 1981).

Tolkien, J.R.R., *The Lost Road and Other Writings: Language and Legend before the Lord of the Rings*, ed. by Christopher Tolkien (London: George Allen & Unwin, 1987).

Tolkien, J.R.R., and Swan, Donald, *The Road Goes Ever On A Song Cycle*, (London: HarperCollins, 2002).

Tolkien, J.R.R., *The Lord of the Rings: The Fellowship of the Ring* (London: HarperCollins, 2005).
—— *The Lord of the Rings: The Two Towers* (London: HarperCollins, 2005).
—— *The Lord of the Rings: The Return of the King* (London: HarperCollins, 2005).
—— 'Tengwesta Qenderinwa and Pre-Fëanorian Alphabets' in *Parma Eldalamberon* XVIII (ed. by Christopher Gilson, Arden R Smith and Patrick H. Wynne, 2009).

Tolkien, J.R.R., *A Secret Vice: Tolkien on Invented Languages*, ed. by Dimitra Fimi and Andrew Higgins (London: HarperCollins, 2016).

"I Heard the Sword's Song, and it Sang to Me": Adapting Tolkien in the World of Heavy Metal

Brian Egede-Pedersen

Introduction

When studying the adaptation (or perhaps even appropriation) of the works of J.R.R. Tolkien, it is quite easy to focus on the film versions of *The Lord of the Rings* and *The Hobbit*, the legacy of Middle-earth in other works of fantasy, role-playing games, etc. Nevertheless, the role of Tolkien's works in the realm of heavy metal is no less interesting or worthy of attention. At first glance, elements traditionally associated with heavy metal such as aggression, overt sexuality, and the darker aspects of humanity do not seem to suit the other Tolkien adaptations, which tend to emphasize the struggle between good and evil, the heroism of the Hobbits and other ordinary folk, or simply the beauty of nature. Indeed, in the first half of the 1990s a small wave of black and death metal bands celebrated the darkest parts of Middle-earth by finding names for themselves or their albums in geographical places connected with evil. Examples include the bands Gorgoroth (Norway, 1992), Amon Amarth, (Sweden, 1992, although they immediately focused on Norse mythology and general Viking themes and iconography instead of the Tolkien legendarium), and Summoning's first three albums: *Lugburz, Minas Morgul*, and *Dol Guldur* (Austria, 1995-1996). Infamously, Norwegian Varg Vikernes based one of his bands (Burzum, 1991, meaning "darkness" in Black Speech) and several songs on Tolkien's writings, not to mention that he took the stage name Count Grishnack [sic] after arguably the most vile and devious Orc that Tolkien created.[1] As a convicted murderer, arsonist, and at the very least an associate of far-right extremist and Neo-Nazi groups, Vikernes is one of the most infamous and studied characters of the metal scene. Nevertheless, this paper turns its attention to a less straightforward example of Tolkien-inspired metal that has received little attention, and will mostly analyze the lesser-known Finnish band Battlelore: How have they adapted Tolkien's universe in their music and lyrics? How much do they know about Middle-earth, and how close are they to Tolkien's original visions? What do heavy metal and the fantasy genre have in common, and how seriously should we take metal lyrics?

---

1. There is something deeply unsettling about Grishnákh, whose voice is described as "Softer than the others but more evil". (*TT*, I, iii) Pippin's recollection of Grishnákh's search for the Ring is eerily similar to that of a sexual assault: "His foul breath was on their cheeks. He began to paw them and feel them. Pippin shuddered as hard cold fingers groped down his back". And "His fingers continued to grope. There was a light like a pale fire behind his eyes." (*TT*, I, iii) When Pippin is to recount the story to Aragorn, Legolas and Gimli during their reunion at Isengard, it is very clear that the young Hobbit is downright traumatized; "He shuddered and said no more, leaving Merry to tell of those last horrible moments: the pawing hands, the hot breath, and the dreadful strength of Grishnákh's hairy arms". (*TT*, I, ix) Since one purpose of black metal often is to shock, provoke, and disgust, it is no great surprise that Vikernes chose to name himself after Grishnákh, as opposed to the more traditional and straightforward brute strength of Uglúk, although one of Vikernes's previous bands was actually called Uruk-hai.

Analysis of Battlelore

Originally founded by guitarist Jyri Vahvanen in 1999, Battlelore released six albums between 2002 and 2011 before going on hiatus, which since then has only been interrupted by infrequent live appearances. From the very beginning, the Tolkien influence is clearly visible: the band's original drummer used the moniker Gorthaur, Sauron's Sindarin name, and their first album was called ...*Where the Shadows Lie*, a part of the inscription on the One Ring.[2] Borrowed from a Ted Nasmith illustration, the album cover for ...*Where the Shadows Lie* depicts the battle between Fingolfin and a highly demonic-looking Morgoth from *The Silmarillion*, mostly focusing on the fallen Ainu. At first glance, everything seems to be as sinister as the already mentioned examples, even more so when the band's second demo was simply named *Dark Fantasy*. A closer look reveals that Battlelore are slightly more difficult to define, both in terms of music and lyrics. Regarding their metal subgenre, it is unusually hard to pigeonhole Battlelore. The band's vocals mostly include the harsh growls often associated with death metal alongside the almost ethereal female vocals typical of symphonic metal, with clean male vocals used intermittently. The music itself is obviously guitar riff-driven and often fast-paced, but frequently with a generally upbeat sound, not least because of an emphasis on the use of keyboards and synthesizers. That a flute is occasionally added, which would normally happen in folk metal, only makes the picture murkier and underlines how the music of Battlelore is quite a genre-

2. The Metal Archives, 'Battlelore', *Encyclopaedia Metallum* <https://www. metal-archives.com/bands/Battlelore/431> [accessed 1 July 2020] (Section: Past Members)

bending concoction: Unlike the deliberately brutal style of black and death metal, the upbeat sound and the subject matter found here point towards power metal, yet as a general rule this subgenre does not use harsh vocals, and Battlelore tend to be less focused on guitar solos and harmonies than traditional power metal bands such as HammerFall and Blind Guardian. The combined "Beauty and the Beast" approach of their vocals could be an indicator of gothic metal, but once again the music is too upbeat for this, while not being quite "symphonic" enough to be comparable to symphonic metal giants like Nightwish and Within Temptation. The band themselves seem aware of the difficulties of pinpointing their genre and have referred to their music as "fantasy metal".[3] The reason why I bring this up is not to dive into the heated subgenre discussions so typical of the metal community, but because the band's lyrics also are quite multifaceted and present many different points of view.

Since it is not possible to analyze everything by Battlelore due to the available space of this paper, three songs from their second album, *Sword's Song* from 2003, are the main focus. This choice was made for a number of reasons: for instance, *Sword's Song* was included in the German metal magazine *EMP*'s Top 25 Albums of the Year and marked a minor breakthrough for Battlelore, probably not least because the time around 2003 witnessed the height of the Tolkien craze ignited by Peter Jackson's *The Lord of the Rings* movies. In addition, this also seems to have been one of the most ambitious periods for the band, with 2004 marking an appearance at the RingCon convention and the release of their only DVD, *The Journey*.

---

3. Luci Herbert, 'Interview with Battlelore', *Metal Team UK*, (2007) <https://web.archive.org/web/20121203045437/http://www.metalteamuk.net/interview-battlelore.htm> [accessed 1 July 2020]

Mostly, however, *Sword's Song* shows an interesting diversity in Battlelore's musical approaches, and practically every song is based on something easily recognizable, unlike some of their later albums which stopped explicitly using names from the Tolkien legendarium:

1. 'Sons of Riddermark'
2. 'Sword's Song'
3. 'The Mark of the Bear'
4. 'Buccaneers Inn'
5. 'Attack of the Orcs'
6. 'Dragonslayer'
7. 'Khazad-Dûm Pt.2 (Silent Caverns)'
8. 'Horns of Gondor' (instrumental)
9. 'The War of Wrath'
10. 'Forked Height'
11. 'Starlight Kingdom'

Evidently, the songs tend to focus on warfare, span mostly the First and the Third Ages, and display more than just a passing knowledge of the stories of Middle-earth. For instance, the chorus of 'Forked Height' shows an awareness of the triple meanings of the word "Orthanc," while 'The Mark of the Bear' refers to the Beornings as "Yavanna's Child",[4] tying together two entities both closely associated with nature. Combined, this indicates far more than just having watched the Peter Jackson movies or a cursory reading of *The Lord of the Rings*. As an aside, Battlelore's third album, aptly

---

4. Battlelore, 'The Mark of the Bear', *Sword's Song*. (Eisenertz: Napalm Records, 2003), fourth verse.

named *Third Age of the Sun*, features songs about the two Blue Wizards, specifically naming them Alatar and Pallando. Apparently, main lyricist Vahvanen either heavily browsed Internet fora or read *Unfinished Tales*. In a 2014 interview, Vahvanen stated: "I found Tolkien's books long before metal conquered my heart",[5] which appears to be reflected in how the covered aspects transcend normal fan knowledge of Tolkien's works. However, to return to *Sword's Song*, I have chosen to take a closer look at three different songs from the album, namely 'Buccaneers Inn', 'Attack of the Orcs' and 'The War of Wrath'. My main analytical points will especially include which groups the listener is supposed to identify with through the narrative style, since identification is a common trope in metal music.

'Buccaneers Inn' is characterized by an unusually upbeat atmosphere, even by Battlelore's standards, with the keyboards providing almost sea shanty-like associations. Indeed, the song is quite nautical as it tells the story of one of the minor villainous factions of Middle-earth, namely the Corsairs of the Haven of Umbar. The lyrics do not show any signs of the dark magic of the Black Númenóreans often connected with Umbar, but instead presents a rather typical, romanticized view of pirates in the vein of, say, the *Pirates of the Caribbean* franchise, which premiered shortly after the release of *Sword's Song*. An example of this view may be seen in the following quotation:

> Open your barrels
> Bring me your finest wine
> Where are the women?
> Your heroes have arrived

5. 'Tolkien in Metal' in *Metal Hammer Magazine*, 252 (2014), pp. 68ff.

64

No sleep tonight my friends
It's time for the pleasures[6]

It is noteworthy that the unnamed speaker of the song is in the first person and, accordingly, tells everything from the Corsairs' point of view. This literary technique invites the listener to identify with the pirates, perhaps even more so when the speaker comes across as tough, confident, and boastful, if somewhat stereotypically masculine and sexist in these lines. Speaking of gender, it should also be noted that female singer Kaisa Jouhki chimes in with a few lines about wanting to dance, drink, and sin.[7] The overall impression of the Corsairs is clearly meant to be positive, even when they boss around their slaves, with the lyrics actually attempting to explain the desire to celebrate:

Fill my mug, I just want to forget
All the troubles and fighting
And the ghosts in my head[8]

In these lines, the Corsairs appear in a nearly sympathetic light as PTSD-struck warriors wishing to drown their sorrows and feelings of regret. Nevertheless, this feeling quickly passes as the already-mentioned lines about dancing and drinking appear, and the chorus repeats "Tonight we will celebrate". As anyone who has had a chance to look at *Songs for the Philologists* will hopefully agree, despite Tolkien being no stranger to

---

6. Battlelore, 'Buccaneers Inn', *Sword's Song*. (Eisenertz: Napalm Records, 2003) second verse.

7. 'Buccaneers Inn', third verse.

8. Ibid.

celebratory drinking songs, this portrayal of the Corsairs does seem to be quite far from what he intended, especially as it takes the side of the antagonists.

Unlike 'Buccaneers Inn', 'Attack of the Orcs' is not told from the point of view of any villain. In terms of pronouns, the Orcs are defined as "our enemies", and they are always referred to as "they", showing no intention of identification on behalf of the listener. Instead, the song seems to be a warning or call to arms to the Free Folk of Middle-earth, as seen in these lines following the second verse, sung by clean male vocals:

Men of Gondor! Elves of Lothlorien!
Dwarves from the north now be strong!
Keep your lines and hold on tight!
Prepare your weapons and strike![9]

The use of the second person, the imperative, and the exclamation marks emphasizes how this is a direct address in a dire situation. Hope is fading, which is seen a few lines later when the defenders are told to "Feel no fear, just pray".[10] A closer look at the aggressively growled chorus reveals why it is so vital for these peoples to defend themselves against the savage onslaught of the Orcs:

They shall raze your villages, destroy your camps
Rape your cattle and slaughter your wives
Under the darkness they shall arrive
Hear the screams, prepare for war

---

9. Battlelore, 'Attack of the Orcs', *Sword's Song*. (Eisenertz: Napalm Records, 2003), third verse.
10. 'Attack of the Orcs', fourth verse.

Black skin, sharp teeth, bestial eyes
Perverted mind, there's no one like their kind
No mercy, no prisoners, death is their way
With fire and steel they will slay[11]

In particular, the second line seems especially grotesque with the deliberate switch of the verbs "rape" and "slaughter", underlining just how degenerate, dangerous and inhuman the Orcs are. In addition, it is impossible to ignore how "black skin" is simply lumped together with all of the horrendous examples of Orcish behaviour. Of course, especially in *The Lord of the Rings*, non-white appearance tends to be associated with something evil, such as the "swart, slant-eyed"[12] Isengarders and the "sallow skin and sly, slanting eyes"[13] of Bill Ferny's southerner friend, or the fighters from Far Harad described as "black men like half-trolls with white eyes and red tongues".[14] This begs the question: Should 'Attack of the Orcs' be interpreted as a statement or warning against non-European immigration? After all, the 1990s had seen right-wing politics gain ground in the Nordic countries with several populist political parties formed, including the True Finns. The years following 9/11 2001 only saw an exacerbated anti-immigration discourse, and lately Finland has been the birthplace of several far-right groups, e.g., the Soldiers of Odin. Nevertheless, I have found no ties between the members of Battlelore and any far-right groups, and in an interview, Vahvanen flatly denies that

---

11. 'Attack of the Orcs', chorus.

12. *TT*, I, i & iii.

13. *FR*, I, xi.

14. *RK*, I, vi.

they have any political messages at all.[15] Patrik Mennander, who was the lead singer on *Sword's Song* and left the band shortly afterwards was also involved with the band Natsipaska,[16] which literally translated from Finnish means "Nazi s**t". Natsipaska are deliberately comedic, and in 2017 they put a picture of several members of Soldiers of Odin on one of their most ridiculous songs.[17] It is possible that the problematic line about "black skin" was not explicitly intended to be perceived as racist, and the inclusion of it does seem like an anomaly when compared to the lyrics of the band's numerous other songs. During a softer part towards the end of 'Attack of the Orcs', a brief thought does speculate about how tortured the existence of an Orc must be: "What kind of evil that they have seen, Can't imagine the pain what they feel".[18] Nevertheless, the chorus is then repeated, and just like in 'Buccaneers Inn', we return to the main focus of the song as the Orcs strike once again. Darkness takes the centre stage here, but unlike in black metal, this is not to be celebrated.

The final example, 'The War of Wrath' is quite a contrast to the two others as it concerns itself with the combined forces of light and goodness finally defeating Morgoth towards the end of the First Age. This epic battle is described as

15. Battlelore, 'Interview with Jyri Vahvanen.', *The Journey*. (Eisenertz: Napalm Records, 2004) 3:35.

16. The Metal Archives, 'Patrik Mennander', *Encyclopaedia Metallum* <https://www.metal-archives.com/artists/Patrik_Mennander/12640> [accessed 1 July 2020] (Section: Past Bands)

17. Natsipaska, 'Natsipaskaa', *Bandcamp* <https://natsipaska.bandcamp.com/track/natsipaskaa> [accessed 1 July 2020]

18. 'Attack of the Orcs', fifth verse.

> Guardians of the world
> Gods of justice and light
> Came and defeated the one
> The master of disharmony[19]

In other words, order is restored to the realm, and everything is set right once more. Unlike the two first songs, there are no first-person pronouns here: the Host of the Valar are referred to in the third person. Whereas 'Attack of the Orcs' used the same literary device to create a distance and underline the inhumanity of the Orcs, here it serves to emphasize the otherworldliness of the armies of light. The listener is not meant to identify with these awe-inspiring beings, as they are portrayed in a verse sung twice by soft, female vocals and accompanied by a musical crescendo:

> All ablaze by the glory of their arms
> Swell of the trumpets filled the sky
> Morgoth banished from the Middle-earth
> His reign never shall rise again[20]

The impression given here is joyful, proud, and triumphant. Good has vanquished evil in limitless glory. While this point of view of the struggle between good and evil may be interpreted as a more optimistic version of the one found in 'Attack of the Orcs', it is most certainly at odds with the romanticized and sympathetic portrayal of the Corsairs of Umbar. Showing the story from such vastly different sides and celebrating both

---

19. Battlelore, 'The War of Wrath', *Sword's Song*. (Eisenertz: Napalm Records, 2003), third verse.

20. 'The War of Wrath', fourth verse.

heroes and villains is a general trait of Battlelore, which begs the question: How is possible to skip back and forth between so dissimilar angles when adapting the works of Tolkien?

The Enchanted Zone

One of the most useful and most applicable terms I have found to explain the fantasy genre is "The Enchanted Zone", coined by Swedish anthropologist Lotten Gustafsson after her studies of the annual Medieval Week on Gotland. Gustafsson noticed that when attendees of the festival dressed up and pretended to be inhabitants of the Middle Ages within the city walls of Visby, they actually acted differently, often without consciously giving it any thought. According to Gustafsson, such situations create a "play chronotope"[21] – a specifically defined time and place (chronos and topos) where normal rules are suspended, and participants are allowed to engage in behaviour that is perhaps not normally accepted, simply because everyone involved agrees with an often unsaid statement: We are just playing, and when that is over, we return to normal life, probably a bit happier than before we began the game.

Perhaps unsurprisingly, at least some members of Battlelore come from a role-playing background or attend live-action role-playing.[22] The booklet accompanying their first album not only included photos of the band members in costume, but also gave them individual Middle-earth character names along with typical role-playing traits such as race, profession, and weapon. This may explain why their lyrics are able to move quickly from one point of view from one song to the next: It is

---

21. Lotten Gustafsson, *Den förtrollade zonen. Leker med tid, rum och identitet under medeltidsveckan på Gotland.* (Nora: Nya Doxa, 2002), pp. 210ff.

22. 'Interview with Jyri Vahvanen', 2:00.

a temporary mask, removed once the song or performance is over, and then you move on to a new role in the game, which all makes sense within the make-believe of the play chronotope. In addition, Vahvanen states that one of the band's goals is to inspire the listener and kindle their imagination: "If you listen carefully, you can see yourself in the [sic] Tolkien's Middle-earth, riding a white horse on the green fields of Rohan".[23] This sort of escapism and feeling of empowerment is quite typical for several metal subgenres, including power metal, which Battlelore resembles in several ways. In that way, heavy metal itself becomes a kind of fantasy, giving the participant the opportunity to dream themselves away into a different world that is "wide and deep and high and filled with many things" where one might "count himself fortunate to have wandered", to use Tolkien's own words (*OFS*, 27), which are not too far from Gustafsson's observations. Metal lyrics should not necessarily be taken at face value, especially regarding violence and warfare. Just like most video games and many aspects of role-playing, heavily emphasizing the martial aspects tends to be a means to focusing on the action leading to that feeling of temporary empowerment, not necessarily a goal in itself. The vast majority of metal (and fantasy) consumers are perfectly aware that when the music stops, the concert ends, the last page of the book is turned, the costumes are removed, the end credits roll, or the game is completed, you leave the enchanted zone. The problem arises when some, like the black metal examples such as Vikernes in the beginning of this paper, do not return to normal life. As Gustafsson said, with a hint of a warning: "You cannot live in an enchanted zone".[24]

Vahvanen was once asked how he thought Tolkien would

---

23. Battlelore, 'Music Video: Grey Wizard', *The Journey*. (Eisenertz: Napalm Records, 2004), 1:45.

24. Gustafsson, p. 252.

have reacted to the music of Battlelore, to which he rather honestly replied: "Oh my god! (Laughs) I think he wouldn't like it".[25] This is probably true, although Tolkien might have appreciated that Battlelore managed to weave the Finnish language into several of their songs. It is also worth noting that although Tolkien was no role-player in the modern sense, he understood the concept of enchanted zones and could readily dress up as an axe-wielding Anglo-Saxon warrior[26] or "turn a lecture room into a mead hall in which he was the bard and we were the feasting listening guests",[27] to quote one of his former students. In the wide world of adapting Tolkien, Battlelore is probably only a footnote, but "Tolkien metal" has its part to play alongside video and tabletop games along with roleplaying to remind us that the legacy of J.R.R. Tolkien keeps taking on its own, sometimes wildly independent life as Middle-earth continues to inspire and fascinate. To quote the signature song of German power metal giants Blind Guardian, whose 1998 concept album *Nightfall in Middle-Earth* was based on *The Silmarillion* and has received its fair share of attention, even scholarly:

> They're always in my mind
> These songs of Hobbits, Dwarves and Men,
> And Elves, come close your eyes
> You can see them too[28]

25. Michael Dalakos, 'Interview with Jyri Vahvanen from Battlelore', *Metal Temple*, (2005) <> [accessed 1 July 2000]

26. Humphrey Carpenter, J.R.R. Tolkien – A Biography (London: Harper Collins, 1996 [1977]), p. 176.

27. Carpenter, p. 179.

28. Blind Guardian, 'The Bard's Song – In the Forest', Somewhere Far Beyond (London: Virgin Records, 1992), third verse.

Bibliography

Battlelore, *Sword's Song* (Eisenertz: Napalm Records, 2003).
--- *The Journey* (Eisenertz: Napalm Records, 2004).

Blind Guardian, *Somewhere Far Beyond* (London: Virgin Records, 1992).

Carpenter, Humphrey, *J.R.R. Tolkien – A Biography* (London: Harper Collins, 1996 [1977]).

Dalakos, Michael, 'Interview with Jyri Vahvanen from Battlelore', *Metal Temple*, (2005) <http://www.metal-temple.com/site/catalogues/entry/musicians/jyri_vahvanen.htm> [accessed 1 July 2000].

Tolkien, J.R.R., *Tolkien On Fairy-Stories* ed. by Verlyn Fliegerand Douglas A. Andersen (London: HarperCollins, 2008).

Gustafsson, Lotten, *Den fortröllade zonen. Leker med tid, rum och identitet under medeltidsveckan på Gotland* (Nora: Nya Doxa, 2002).

Herbert, Luci, 'Interview with Battlelore', *Metal Team UK*, (2007) <https://web.archive.org/web/20121203045437/http://www.metalteamuk.net/interview-battlelore.htm> [accessed 1 July 2020].

The Metal Archives, 'Battlelore', *Encyclopaedia Metallum* <https://www.metal-archives.com/bands/Battlelore/431> [accessed 1 July 2020].
—— 'Patrik Mennander', *Encyclopaedia Metallum* <https://www.metal-archives.com/artists/Patrik_Mennander/12640> [accessed 1 July 2020].

Metal Hammer, 'Tolkien in Metal' in *Metal Hammer Magazine*, 252 (2014).
Natsipaska, 'Natsipaskaa', *Bandcamp* <https://natsipaska.bandcamp.com/track/natsipaskaa> [Accessed on 1 July 2020].

Tolkien, J.R.R., *The Fellowship of the Ring* (London: HarperCollins, 2007 [1954]).
—— *The Two Towers* (London: HarperCollins, 2007 [1954]).
—— *The Return of the King* (London: HarperCollins, 2007[1955]).

Is Adapting Tolkien (Mis)Remembering Tolkien?

Mina D. Lukić

'In the workings of the human imagination, adaptation is the norm, not the exception.'[1]

These closing words of Linda Hutcheon's seminal book *A Theory of Adaptation* point to the fact that adaptations have had a long history of presence and popularity in Western culture. For most of that history, attitude towards them was positive rather than negative, which is often forgotten in the case of literature-to-film adaptations. The nature of derogatory attitudes toward such adaptations is briefly examined before we tackle the question of adaptations and memory, and whether adapting Tolkien means remembering or misremembering Tolkien (or both in some instances). Topics concerning literature and memory, as well as film and memory, have gained a decent amount of scholarly attention, but extraordinarily little has been said about film adaptations of fantasy literature from the perspective of cultural memory studies.[2] Thus, the aim of this

2. Notable exception being Colin B. Harvey, *Fantastic Transmedia. Narrative, Play and Memory Across Science Fiction and Fantasy Storyworlds* (London: Palgrave Macmillan, 2015). Further references to this edition are given in parentheses.

paper is to offer some ideas and insights on Peter Jackson's film adaptations of Tolkien's novels in the context of individual and collective memory.

Three types of memory are distinguished in memory studies: individual, social, and cultural memory. Individual memory is our personal memory dependent on our neuro-mental system. Although personal, this memory is always realised within sociocultural contexts, i.e., relies on collective memory. Communicative/social memory is a form of collective memory which rests upon communication and social interaction, it is a so-called generational memory which usually has 'the time span of three interacting generations', and it is not formalised and stabilised through institutions or material forms of remembrance. Such media-supported and stabilised form of collective memory, embodied in monuments, museums, libraries, archives, and other mnemonic objects and institutions, able to outlast many generations, is what we call cultural memory.[3] These three levels of memory make up the ways in which Tolkien and his works are remembered, and we will discuss Peter Jackson's adaptations in respect of all three.

Adaptations and Memory

There are four interconnected phenomena which lie at the root of all attitudes towards book-to-film adaptations: the

3. Jan Assmann, 'Communicative and Cultural Memory', in *Cultural Memory Studies: An International and Interdisciplinary Handbook*, ed. by Astrid Erll and Ansgar Nünning (Berlin – New York: Walter de Gruyter, 2008), 109–118 (pp. 109–111).

notions of the *original and originality*, the idea of *autonomy of art*, the *fear of images*, and the *issues of memory*. The first two are crucial for the concepts of *priority* and *fidelity* which usually determine the scope of expectations people have from adaptations, and also serve as main arguments in dismissing them, which is reflected in numerous debates surrounding Jackson's film adaptations of Tolkien's works, exclusively centred on the issues of fidelity. The issues of memory derive from imposing the fidelity claim on adaptations – questioning whether they proper-ly remember the story, or misremember, change, challenge, forget, or leave out some parts of it. Coupled with a distrust towards visual media and their presupposed superiority over text, these phenomena underlie most of the debates concerning film adaptations within Tolkien fandom and this paper will take a closer look into all of them.

Nicolas Poussin, one of the most prominent 17th century artists, explained what invention and originality meant in Western art prior to Romanticism: 'The novelty in painting does not consist principally in a new subject, but in good and new disposition and expression, and thus the subject from being common and old becomes singular and new.'[4] Namely, telling the same story in a new way, but 'making the adapted material one's own' (Hutcheon, 20) which can be said to roughly correspond to present-day adapters' intentions. The ideas of artistic creativity and originality as we know them have had their beginnings in the 18th century and were fully

---

4. From Bellori, *Le vite dei pittori*, quoted in Rensselaer W. Lee, 'Ut Pictura Poesis: The Humanistic Theory of Painting', *The Art Bulletin*, Vol. 22, No. 4 (Dec., 1940), 197–269 (pp. 210–211).

formed by the Romantic movement of the late 18th and 19th centuries, largely determining the development of modern art.[5] The romantic notion of originality became one of the dominant discourses of authority in our cul-ture, causing adaptations to be frequently put down as secondary, derivative, and culturally inferior in the last two centuries (Hutcheon, 4).

Romantics also came up with a different idea of what art is/should be, which has shaped the way we think about art to the present day: the idea of *l'art pour l'art* or *art for art's sake*. This concept became a foundation of the *autonomy of art* doctrine, stating that a work of art has an in-trinsic value and should be devoid of any practical function or instrumental value. The authority, autonomy, and integrity of the original work of art thus became and remained unquestionable till Postmodernism. It comes as no surprise that these concepts, crucial in the creation and evaluation of art during the 20th century, are deeply rooted in our collective consciousness and very persistent. Although challenged in postmodern theory and art, the cult status of the author and the 'original' remain strong influences in judging numerous art forms, especially adaptations, where presuppos-ing the supremacy and priority of the 'original' over its interpretations is a commonplace.

Fidelity to the 'original' has for a long time been the main criteria of evaluation of literature-to-film adaptations, usually picturing adaptations in negative terms of loss, whether in quantity or quality (Hutcheon, 37). 21st century adaptation studies have moved beyond fidelity criticism, em-phasising

---

5. See Rosalind Krauss, *The Originality of the Avant-Garde and Other Modernist Myths* (Cambridge, MA – London: The MIT Press, 1986); and Kamilla Elliott, *Theorizing Adaptation*, (New York: Oxford University Press, 2020).

that adaptations are aesthetic objects in their own right and that the proximity to the source text should not be the basis of analysis or judgment.[6] Nonetheless, fidelity continues to be an issue for fans who often focus on how closely an adaptation is faithful to their beloved text, and we will see that that is especially true of many voices in the Tolkien community.

Fidelity criticism ignores the fact that there are many different motives behind adaptation, few involving complete faithfulness to the source text. As Linda Hutcheon pointed out, 'the urge to con-sume and erase the memory of the adapted text or to call it into question is as likely as the desire to pay tribute by copying' (Hutcheon, 7). Said urge to consume and erase the memory of the adapted text points to the importance of memory in the context of adaptations. The constant criticism litera-ture-to-film adaptations receive as inferior to the 'original' and the fear of them rely on the idea that they aim and are able to corrupt/replace/erase the original memory of a book:

> The adaptation trades upon the memory of the novel, a memory that can derive from actual reading, or, as is more likely with a classic of literature, a generally circulated cultural memory. The adaptation consumes this memory, aiming to efface it with the presence of its own images. The successful adaptation is one that is able to replace the memory of the novel with the process of a filmic or televisual representation.[7]

---

6. Hutcheon, *Preface*, p. XXVI, p. 6; Elliott, pp. 139–171; Martin Barker, 'Envisaging "Visualisation": Some challenges from the international *Lord of the Rings* project', *Film–Philosophy*, v. 10, n. 3 (2006), 1–25 (p. 6). Further references to this text are given in parentheses.
7. John Ellis, 'The Literary Adaptation', *Screen*, Vol. 23, Issue 1 (May/June 1982), 3–5 (p. 3).

The quotation above indicates a widespread attitude that film images are able to take over a text and replace a memory of a novel. The ambiguity over the power of images and their suggestiveness, a belief that they can 'seduce and lead us astray' has been one of the constants in human history, with film as a medium making it only more obvious.[8] Hence, film adaptations are frequently accused of being able to 'interrupt or spoil imaginative processes set underway by book-reading' (Barker, 6). This fear of images and their power is in many instances exaggerated, but we will see that it is a persistent concern among Tolkien fans, many of them regretting the influence of Jack-son's films on their visualisation of Middle-earth, and some of them completely avoiding the films in order not to compromise their own vision of the world. In contrast with some previous attempts of showing *The Lord of the Rings* and *The Hobbit* on screen, Jackson's film adaptations have been highly successful and visually impressive, which made them appear more dangerous to people who fear that they could replace the memory of the books.

Memory is the source of both fear of adaptations and their appeal. Experiencing adaptations *as adaptations* is grounded in memory: it requires previous knowledge of the adapted work, if there is none, the work is not experienced as an adaptation. In order to be successful, an adaptation must stand on its own and tell the story for both knowing and unknowing audiences (Hutcheon, 121). Yet, it has a special appeal for knowing audiences, which lies in experiencing the stories they love in a new way, with constant oscillation between an

---

8. W. J. T. Mitchell, What Do Pictures Want. *The Lives and Loves of Images* (Chicago and London: The University of Chicago Press, 2005), p. 19.

adapted work and its adaptation. The pleasure aris-es from intertextual and intermedial juxtapositions between the two, from experiencing them at the same time and understanding their interplay.[9] In this process, memory is essential 'in order to expe-rience difference as well as similarity' (Hutcheon, 22) and it can be the cause of both pleasure and frustration. When experiencing an adaptation, we fill in the gaps with information from the adapted text based on our knowledge and memory, and our level of satisfaction usually depends on the amount of similarity we expect compared to our own vision. All three (our knowledge, memory, and our vision of a fictional world) are highly individual and subjective.

Subjective Interpretations and Great Expectations

Reception theory and fandom studies help us understand how people relate to Tolkien's imaginary world and how they make sense of its interpretations in different media, which is crucial for explaining Tolkien's relevance today, and, consequently, his lasting presence in our collective memory. It is about understanding fans and fan communities because they add new values to Tolkien's stories and enable them to last, be relevant and remembered – they are creators and guardians of a living memory. Therefore, we will first consider fans' attitudes towards different interpretations of Tolkien's works in order to understand their expectations.

When reconstructing any fictional world in our minds, we rely on our abilities of interpretation, memory, and imagination.

9. Hutcheon, p. 116; Henry Jenkins, *Textual Poachers: Television Fans and Participatory Culture* (London – New York: Routledge, 1992), p. 37. Further references to this edition are given in parentheses.

The way we understand and interpret things, as well as the way we remember and imagine them, is determined by our cultural background, our value systems, our knowledge and mental abilities, our personal interests, and taste. When evaluating an adaptation of the work we love, we operate in a context which includes all this, as well as our knowledge, our memory, and our own interpretation of the source text (Hutcheon, 111). As such, we all imagine Tolkien's world in at least slightly different ways. The need to emphasise this comes from the fact that individuals frequently forget it, which is inherent to our way of thinking – we naturally assume that others see and understand the world in the same manner as we do.[10] When our perspective is challenged, we feel threatened, and the more emotionally invested we are, the more defensive our reaction will be. Fan identity is largely grounded in an emotional investment and a sense of ownership, which is why fan communities often have difficulties arriving at a consensus about proper treatment of the stories they love. The field of interpretation often becomes a field of heated debates, in many instances initiated by fidelity claims and insisting that only one interpretation is possible. That is rarely the case, especially when the works as complex as Tolkien's are at stake, and even less so when it comes to their adaptations. Becoming aware of subjectivity and relativity of interpretation on an individual level is the first step towards a better understanding of ourselves, of others, and of the works of fiction we hold dear, as well as towards creating more tolerant communication spaces within Tolkien fandom.

---

10. For this phenomenon, named *false consensus effect*, see: Lee Ross, David Greene, Pamela House, 'The "False Consensus Effect": An Egocentric Bias in Social Perception and Attribution Processes', *Journal of Experimental Social Psychology*, Volume 13, Issue 3 (May 1977), 279–301.

There are multiple ways in which authors, fans and other interested parties try to control and negotiate the subjective and collective interpretation and remembering of a certain story. Fandoms are broadly defined as interpretative communities of individuals connected by love and admiration for a particular content; they have some shared experience and knowledge, and create social structures, rituals, and traditions of their own.[11] For many people, being a fan involves the need to belong to a community of like-minded individuals, the desire to share personal opinions, feelings and visions of a beloved story, and compare them with other people's interpretations. It is a social process through which cultural canons are constructed and individual interpretations 'shaped and reinforced through ongoing discussions with other readers' (Jenkins, 45–46). Belonging to such a community 'can heighten our sense of excitement, prompt our self-reflexivity, encourage us to discuss shared values and ethics, and supply us with a significant source of meaning that extends into our daily lives' (Duffett, 50).

That being said, in order to illustrate fans' attitudes towards various interpretations of Tolkien's works and the scope of expectations they have from adaptations, we will refer to some of the results of 6 surveys I have conducted in the last three years (4 international and 2 in Serbia), with the total of 3,115 participants from over 90 countries. Most of the respondents (over 89%) have both read the books and watched the films (Chart 1). My own results largely correspond with many conclusions drawn from several big international film audience

11. Mark Duffett, *Understanding Fandom. An Introduction to the Study of Media Fan Culture* (New York – London: Bloomsbury, 2013), p. 48. Further references to this edition are given in parentheses.

research projects and I will occasionally refer to them, but primarily use my own surveys to illustrate the points made.[12]

See Chart 1 (right).

To begin with, in one of my surveys[13] which was conceived as an interview, with in-depth open-ended questions, targeting a small group of people (31 respondents so far), participants were asked: 'Do you think that anyone can and should interpret Tolkien's works in accordance with their own vision? What attitude do you have towards interpretations that drastically deviate from the books?' The indicative answers were:

1. No, I do not agree at all with people who choose to interpret Tolkien's works in such a far-fetched way that is completely unrelated to the works and their original meaning.

---

12. *The Lord of the Rings World Audience Project* database is available at https://pure.aber.ac.uk/portal/en/datasets/lord-of-the-rings-world-audience-database(b403222b-74b6-4686-9cc6-dfd1de16a31a).html, for *The World Hobbit Project* database see https://pure.aber.ac.uk/portal/en/datasets/the-world-hobbit-project-database(aa40f8e7-00d3-45dd-b63b-e5da58168312). html. A number of papers have been published following both projects, the largest collections being *Watching the Lord of the Rings: Tolkien's World Audiences*, ed. by Martin Barker and Ernest Mathijs (New York: Peter Lang, 2008) and a special issue of the journal *Participations* (Vol. 13:2, 2016) available at https://www.participations.org/Volume%2013/Issue%202/contents.htm. Also see: Carolyn Michelle, and others, *Fans, Blockbusterisation, and the Transformation of Cinematic Desire: Global Receptions of the Hobbit Film Trilogy*, (London: Palgrave Macmillan, 2017). 13. This survey is available at https://minalukic.wixsite.com/tolkienheritage/wandering-with-tolkien. In all my surveys participants were either anonymous or offered to choose whether they wanted to stay anonymous or have their answers presented under their full name, initials, or pseudonym.

Chart 1. Check the books/films you have read/watched in their entirety:

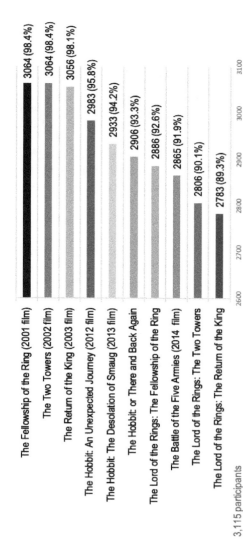

3,115 participants

- The Fellowship of the Ring (2001 film): 3064 (98.4%)
- The Two Towers (2002 film): 3064 (98.4%)
- The Return of the King (2003 film): 3056 (98.1%)
- The Hobbit: An Unexpected Journey (2012 film): 2983 (95.8%)
- The Hobbit: The Desolation of Smaug (2013 film): 2933 (94.2%)
- The Hobbit or There and Back Again: 2906 (93.3%)
- The Lord of the Rings: The Fellowship of the Ring: 2886 (92.6%)
- The Battle of the Five Armies (2014 film): 2865 (91.9%)
- The Lord of the Rings: The Two Towers: 2806 (90.1%)
- The Lord of the Rings: The Return of the King: 2783 (89.3%)

I love to read them for what they are and for what Tolkien intended them to be. They do not need all those strange interpretations I read or hear about all the time, to be magical and worth reading. They can stand on their own and I honestly believe that some of the interpretations out there would make Tolkien cringe. (E.T., 29, UK)

2.   I view them as new works, curiously lacking in original content; lazy world building; possibly self indulgent. (Karen Wolf, Australia, 47)

3.   Due to my deep understanding and love for Tolkien's work I am very skeptical of others' interpretations. I don't tolerate those that deviate drastically from the canon. (Jelena Filipovic, 28, Germany)

4.   Some people find there things that the author never mentioned, it is ok if you present is just as a personal opinion, but not if you present it as a fact (I think of you, Day!) (Martina Juričková, Slovakia, 29)

5.   Privately, yes – I have a long history of playing Middle-earth (tabletop) RPGs whose plot elements may deviate drastically from Tolkien. But I feel quite contemptuous towards deviations from the canon when I come across them in public, whether it be a game or a tumblr fanon. (Maria Talvela, 30, Finland)

6.   Can? Yes, anyone can do that. The trick is to avoid it. Should? No. The post-modern "death of the author" is one of the huge mistakes, and, to my mind, mostly expresses a very unhealthy self-absorption. The author, and the author's intention, is the only common ground we have – our only unbiased interpretation – to stand upon when discussing literature. It is unavoidable that our personal history will interfere with our reading, but the ideal should nonetheless be the unbiased interpretation, and we should strive to suppress our selves in the understanding of another human mind (crucial for empathy, active listening and critical thinking).

Consequently, I tend to dismiss interpretations that drastically deviate from Tolkien's known intentions as mistaken and uninteresting – just so much nonsensical noise. (T.F., 54, Denmark)

7. Every interpretation needs an argument to follow and I don't think that personal feelings are a strong enough argument (generally in life). However, I am really interested in learning how someone from different background than mine understood parts of the story when experiencing it for the first time, because all is filtered by our mindset and personal history. Nevertheless, the story was written in a context and I do not think anyone has the right to force their own vision as equally correct when scholars and fans can check how the story evolved in other Tolkien's works. (K.W., Poland, 30)

8. I think that Tolkien's works can be interpreted by anyone, but the validity of that interpretation may differ. For example, there is widespread popularity for introducing LGBT+ themes or explaining why some characters 'are' LGBT+ in Middle-earth. While this is one interpretation, and one I can appreciate as a member of the LGBT+ community, I also know that Tolkien did not write any queer characters into his books and this interpretation has no wider validity. In comparison to this, there are interpretations that feed off the various story lines that Tolkien wrote before the final draft (Amras burning in Losgar etc.) and I think these hold more validity because they are tied to the greater narrative of Middle-earth. (H.H.B., 21, Canada)

9. I think anyone should be allowed to interpret any work as they wish; however, I do not think all interpretations are equally valid. The more they deviate from the books, the less value they hold for me. (M.J., Slovenia, 38)

10. Every person experiences each book or film differently. If something does not deviate from the core (morality and philosophy) of Tolkien's works, it doesn't bother me. (V.Č.N., 45, Serbia)

11. Yes, I think they can, and it's not for me to say they shouldn't. When it comes to interpretations that drastically deviate from the books, I'm probably not going to be interested in them, but that doesn't mean they shouldn't exist. If they have meaning for someone, then I'm not going to tell them they are wrong. (Sally Kennett, 48, UK)

12. I think anyone should be allowed to do anything. An interpretation is always based on someone's experiences or knowledge. Sometimes one might go too far but still it is important to see someone doing so. By exploring the extreme sometimes you might unearth something quite subtle in the original. It would be fascinating to have such a revelation or expose others to it unknowingly. (Sofia Athanasopoulou, 22, Greece)

13. I don't think that any two people have the same interpretation of Tolkien's works, sometimes this has lead to arguments (i.e. Balrogs and wings). Because Tolkien was inspired by so many different cultures and beliefs and they were all added into his 'cooking pot' in some way, different parts will stand out and mean different things to different people. One of the most incredible things about Tolkien's works is that it means different things to different people. I think any interpretation is a valid interpretation, no matter how much it deviates from the book. Just because it doesn't accurately represent the books, doesn't mean that the interpretation isn't enjoyable in its own right. Again, as far as I'm concerned, any adaptation or interpretation that helps to spread the love of Tolkien's works is a good thing, even if it is inaccurate. (Karl Southern, 23, UK)

It was possible to discern three types of attitudes among 31 'knowing audience' participants: first one, extremely negative towards interpretations, considering them an unnecessary spoiling or uncreative feeding off the original (7 answers); second, moderate attitude allowing for interpretations which retain the spirit of the original and do not deviate seriously from the books (15); and finally, a positive view supporting the variety of interpretations as a means of promoting Tolkien and discovering or generating new meanings that circulate around the primary text (9).

The first group had an almost sacrosanct respect towards the books, and often used the strict fidelity claim as the only evaluation criteria. The second group required a general faithfulness to the spirit of the world and the essence of the story. The last group welcomed all interpretations as creative works expressing different visions and inspiring people to approach the original from new perspectives. The participants mostly considered that anyone may interpret Tolkien's works, but that it does not mean that they would be interested in said interpretations, especially if they seriously deviated from the books. However, even the ones who were against such interpretations and not interested in them, often realised that they can bring new people into Tolkien's fictional world and get them intrigued to further explore it.

The participants with a positive view of interpretations were the ones who also engaged in reading fan fiction (8) or in creating Tolkien-inspired content (10). They had no difficulty in separating the source material from the content it inspired, which clearly shaped their expectations and attitudes towards other people's interpretations. As Karl Southern put it 'Just because it doesn't accurately represent the books, doesn't mean that the interpretation isn't enjoyable in its own right.' (comment no. 13 above).

Notwithstanding, the answer of Maria Talvela (no. 5

above) appropriately highlights the ambiguity of assessing personal visions against other people's interpretations of Tolkien's fiction. It goes to show that subjective visions, usually constructed as a blend of various sources and influences, are central to individual pleasure, and while it can be acceptable to deviate from the 'canon' privately, similar deviations are rejected when encountered in public. As Colin Harvey recognised, 'discussions regarding issues of canon frequently illustrate ongoing tensions between the relationship of subjective remembering and collective memory, even leading to the oxymoronic concept of "personal canon", i.e. an individual's subjective opinion on what constitutes the collective "reality" of the storyworld' (Harvey, 4) also labelled 'headcanon'. This reveals that for many aficionados of Tolkien, being a fan represents a complex private yet shared experience which requires constant negotiation between subjective visions and collective norms, a process which applies to evaluation of adaptations too.

Several participants stressed that personal taste and individual visions are not above facts, questioning validity of interpretations which drastically deviate from the books and affirming the adherence to the 'canon' as desirable or necessary. Thus, the majority of respondents were not fond of interpretations which did not 'remember' their beloved source material correctly or drastically altered the core and spirit of the story, which goes to confirm that the enduring appeal of adaptations, as well as our frustration with them, lies in the dynamics of recognition and remembrance inherent in the adaptation process (Hutcheon, 4, 21) and that adaptations are more likely to produce a pleasurable viewing if they are sufficiently aligned with participants' memory of the books.

In order to further situate Jackson's adaptations in the context of memory, we will have a closer look into audience attitudes towards differences between the books and the films and their impact on individual remembering of the story, as well as their effect on people's visualisation of Middle-earth, before considering their role in our collective remembering of Tolkien and his works.

(Mis)Remembering the Story

Both fans and adapters have deeply personal reasons for being attracted to Tolkien, and as we cannot expect that our personal vision will correspond with everyone else's, we also cannot expect that any adaptation should be a literal translation or a perfect copy of the original. Adapting is both interpretation and creation, where adapters take possession of a story, and recreate it in accordance with their own sensibility, interests, and talents (Hutcheon, 8, 18, 111). In the process, they choose to remember with fidelity or knowingly misremember some elements of the story to suit their creative aims. 'Recognition and remembrance are part of the pleasure (and risk) of experiencing an adaptation; so too is change.' (Hutcheon, 4), and some changes introduced by the adapters are created in order to make the stories more relevant for us in the present, not with the intention of 'ruining' the original. Ironically, when not judged based on their fidelity to the source material, adapters can be accused of not sufficiently referring to some contemporary topics, e.g., the issues of race, gender, disability, post-colonialism, etc.[14]

According to my research, the number of people appreciative of *The Lord of the Rings* adaptations significantly surpasses the ones who see them as a debasement of Tolkien's work, however, Jackson and his team have been accused of both corrupting the original and of not paying proper attention to some contemporary concerns. At the same time, the efforts to appeal to contemporary audiences' tastes, values, and experiences can be seen as a serious degradation of the original, which is a frequent criticism of *The Hobbit* trilogy. To put it simply, a perfect adaptation that would please everyone does not exist, but the diverse answers my respondents gave when asked what they thought of Jackson's film adaptations, illustrate the complexity of their reception:

1.   I think the LotR movies are really well done. You can't of course convey all the meaning and the stories of the books in the movies, but I think they did a good job. (I.A., Italy, 25)

2.   I loved Jackson's adaptations, I don't necessarily think that they were good as an adaptation, but they pulled me in from a young age. I'm less keen on his Hobbit films, but I still enjoy watching them as films […] I think the most important adaptations are probably the Jackson films and LOTRO, because its two different mediums and two different versions of the text, both of which draw you in and act as a gateway to Tolkien and his legendarium. (Karl Southern, 23, UK)

14. E.g. see: Daniel Smith-Rowsey, 'Whose Middle-earth is it? Reading *The Lord of the Rings* and New Zealand's New Identity from a Globalized, Post-Colonial Perspective', in *How We Became Middle-earth. A Collection of Essays on The Lord of the Rings*, ed. by Adam Lam and Nataliya Oryshchuk (Zurich and Berne: Walking Tree Publishers, 2007) 129–145.

3.   Generally good, they invite others to explore his work through other mediums. Some people might find reading such a long book difficult but they might get pleasure from watching the films. (L.L., UK, 64)

4.   I LOVE the LOTR films, they have captured the essence of the story. I do find the Hobbit films horrible though. They are just so bad. (E.T., 29, UK)

5.   I think The LOTR trilogy is a good representation of the books. In any case, I think it is as good as it could be, and I always enjoy watching it. There are some 'untolkienesque' jokes, but far fewer than would be expected. The design of The Hobbit is beautiful, and many of the actors were well chosen for their roles, but the writing and the storyline are abysmal. (H.H.B., 21, Canada)

6.   I liked the LOTR trilogy and the first half of the first Hobbit movie, and loathed the two remaining Hobbit films. The reason for my dislike isn't with the added parts in itself (e.g. I think Dol Guldur was well done and also needed, to explain Gandalf's absence), but with bad changes to the existing story (like the mischaracterisation of Smaug, some dwarves staying in Lake Town), added storylines that went nowhere (random talks about Legolas's mother), characters like Alfrid and their version of the mayor (caricature is not a strong enough word for them), and terribly unrealistic action scenes (I know it's fantasy, but this was heavily over the top even for that). (M.J., Slovenia, 38)

7.   My general view is that an adaptation is a work of art by the adapting artist. It is an independent work of art, and the adapting artist should not be obliged to stay 'faithful' to the adapted work in any particular way. Some of the best adaptations that I know of have treated the original with a certain degree of disrespect. Better (in my personal view) adaptations, however, tend to respect the underlying aesthetic and ethical themes of the original [...] Peter Jackson's 'The

Lord of the Rings' trilogy are, in my view, excellent films, but they fail utterly in portraying Tolkien's Middle-earth: visually, ethically, aesthetically, etc. This failure is felt the stronger because they manage to stay close to the surface of the story. Jackson's Hobbit films, however, are horrible as films and also fail to stay close to the surface plot, making it easier to ignore the claimed relation. (T.F., 54, Denmark)

8.   I dislike Peter Jackson's LOTR and detest his Hobbit. (Okay, that was slightly exaggerated, LOTR – I think there are some good things about it but I'm not a fan.) He completely misses the nuances that make Tolkien's writing so captivating and is largely to blame for the black-and-white accusations that Tolkien receives. PJ thinks he can improve on Tolkien's stories and that's not true. (Maria Talvela, 30, Finland)

9.   Peter Jackson's The Lord of the Rings is a worthy adaptation, where a huge effort was made to bring the film closer to the book [...] It seems to me that a film has rarely had such a difficult task as an adaptation, but there was a will not to sink into commercialisation and a desire to create the world that Tolkien would not be ashamed of. So I consider this adaptation a success and I have watched it many times, as well as the accompanying 'making of' discs [...] The Hobbit films are the opposite of all this: subordinated to the commercial, they changed the narrative in key places, introducing banal Hollywood stereotypes, suppressing the meaning of many Tolkien's concepts [...] with numerous bad and unnecessary fabrications added whilst some extraordinary parts of the original story were left out. Of course, there are some good scenes, but unfortunately they are few. (Tatjana Mihailović, Serbia, 56)

10.   Lord of the Rings happened in a time when film was not too commercialised. I feel it was the ideal time for it and it came out well by also making progress on its field

with motion capture and cg animation. Hobbit on the other hand was rushed mainly due to typical Hollywood issues coming from Warner Bros. The balance between cgi and liveaction shifted, action sequences replaced and erased the true meaning of Tolkien's work and were overbearing. Additions of unnecessary characters that shouldn't be there prove the commercial side as well. (Sofia Athanasopoulou, 22, Greece)

11.   Pure abomination. The books should be left unspoiled, unless the director and screenwriter are capable of not missing out on any detail, important or not for the film as a medium. I hope that *The Silmarillion* will never be filmed, because *The Lord of the Rings*, and especially *The Hobbit* were banalised and devalued by filming. (Marko Vasić, 36, Serbia)

12.   I find Jackson's Hobbit very far from the book but also quite incoherent in itself and frequently poorly shot. (Mathilde Samson, France, 33)

These answers highlight most of the issues which arose concerning Jackson's adaptations, including people loving the films and seeing them 'as a gateway to Tolkien and his legendarium', the ones evaluating them positively or negatively on the basis of fidelity or adherence to 'the core of the original', as well as the ones criticising them for banalisation, excessive commercialisation, unnecessary Hollywood influences and changes aimed to appeal to mainstream audiences.

It is not a new insight that the reception of Jackson's adaptations can range from a view that the films are perfect or even 'better' than the books, to fervent complaints that they vandalise the original and miss its essence completely, being designed only to make profit. Such views and similar comments appeared in all my surveys, but more dominant sentiment was a dislike of major deviations from the books which were not adequately explained or justified, jeopardising the meaning of the story and the internal consistency of the storyworld itself. That is probably the most obvious in the comments above where Jackson and his team are praised for being faithful to 'the spirit of the books' in the case of *The Lord of the Rings* trilogy whilst accused of failing to be true to 'the core of the original' with *The Hobbit*.

The problem lies in the fact that what is understood as 'the core of the original' varies and is subject to individual criteria, whether we talk about scholars or fandom in general. Luckily, Tolkien himself pointed out in the letter to Forrest J. Ackerman that the core of *The Lord of the Rings* or 'the heart of the tale' lies in 'the journey of the Ringbearers' (*Letters*, 271). The reason that the first trilogy has so many admirers is that this core of the story has been mostly preserved and properly emphasised, despite all the changes introduced. Altering the storytelling structure to show several storylines happening simultaneously, reducing the time span and taking out the material which would slow down the pace of the film and introduce too many characters into an already complex array of protagonists (e.g. Tom Bombadil), replacing characters like Glorfindel and Erkenbrand with Arwen and Éomer to more fully develop their characters, bringing in the Elves at Helm's Deep to emphasise the idea of unity and show them fighting – these modifications did not change the core story, but were used to focus the audience's attention on the immediate danger the ring represents and give a sense of urgency to the entire quest of destroying it.[15]

More problematic for many people were the omission of the Scouring of the Shire or character changes, e.g., drastically altering Faramir and Denethor; making Gimli more 'amusing'; overemphasising the physical prowess of Legolas, leading to unrealistic action scenes in both trilogies, etc.[16] Some changes were made with the intention of making certain characters responsible for major plot shifts (e.g. Pippin redirecting Treebeard and causing the Ents to fight or lighting the beacons); some were supposed to show heroes' personal journey of overcoming obstacles and temptations; some were build-ups expanding the role of female characters, aimed to keep them

15. For different takes on the subject and an in-depth comparison of *The Lord of the Rings* books and films, see: Tom Shippey, 'Another Road to Middle-earth: Jackson's Movie Trilogy', in *Roots and Branches: Selected Papers on Tolkien* (Zurich and Berne: Walking Tree Publishers, 2007), pp. 365–386, also available as 'Tolkien Book to Jackson Script: the Medium and the Message', a talk delivered at Swarthmore College on 16.2.2010, available at https://www.swarthmore.edu/news-events/tolkien-book-to-jackson-script-medium-and-message. Øystein Høgset, 'The Adaptation of *The Lord of the Rings* – A Critical Comment', in: *Translating Tolkien: Text and Film*, ed. by Thomas Honegger (Zurich and Berne: Walking Tree Publishers, 2004), pp. 165–180. James Dunning, 'The Professor and the Director and Good vs. Evil in Middle-earth', in: *Translating Tolkien: Text and Film*, ed. by Thomas Honegger (Zurich and Berne: Walking Tree Publishers, 2004), pp. 181–212.
16. For the analysis of *The Lord of the Rings* characters in the films, see: Anthony S. Burdge & Jessica Burke, 'Humiliated Heroes: Peter Jackson's Interpretation of *The Lord of the Rings*', in: *Translating Tolkien: Text and Film*, ed. by Thomas Honegger (Zurich and Berne: Walking Tree Publishers, 2004), pp. 135–164; James G. Davis, 'Showing Saruman as Faber: Tolkien and Peter Jackson', *Tolkien Studies*, Volume 5 (2008), 55–71; Judy Ann Ford, Robin Anne Reid, 'Councils and Kings: Aragorn's Journey Towards Kingship in J.R.R. Tolkien's *The Lord of the Rings* and Peter Jackson's *The Lord of the Rings*', *Tolkien Studies*, Volume 6 (2009), 71–90.

present in all three films for the sake of continuity (introducing Evenstar as Arwen's symbolic presence or Aragorn's fall of the cliff during the warg attack ensuring that Arwen appears in the second film). Some characters were simplified, some depicted through a more contemporary lens, and although they usually arrive at the same narrative resolution, their development and narrative arcs are different in the books and the films, e.g., in the case of Aragorn, who is gradually accepting who he is in the films, or Boromir, who was given a more emotional redemption and death than in the books. Jackson wanted to create an emotional interpretation in many instances, another example being Théoden's presence at Théodred's funeral and his statement 'No parent should have to bury their child.', which is completely at odds with the Rohirric notion of death, but effective and resonant with contemporary audiences.

However, all these and other unmentioned modifications in *The Lord of the Rings* trilogy are something which book lovers can notice; they can agree or disagree whether they were necessary, but even when regretting particular changes they are aware that it is impossible to convey everything from the books on screen (comment no. 1 above), and ultimately more inclined to accept or overlook the changes for other qualities this trilogy possesses. That this is not the case with *The Hobbit* films is well summarised by one of the respondents:

> The film adaptations of *The Lord of the Rings* kept the spirit of the books. That is why numerous changes, such as the absence of Tom Bombadil, the elves in Helm's Deep or the depiction of Sauron as a giant fiery eye at the top of the tower, did not bother me much. It's different with *The Hobbit* films, where all Hollywood deficiencies are quite obvious, such as the full

reliance on special effects. I'm not saying that these films do not have any quality at all, but there are too many flaws which cannot be ignored. (Stefan Jovanović, 31, Serbia)

The majority of the participants considered the second trilogy to be a poor adaptation, amounting to 'pure abomination', and the frequency of rewatching *The Hobbit* films turned out to be drastically lower than in the case of *The Lord of the Rings*. In the letter mentioned above, Tolkien himself warned that: 'The canons of narrative art in any medium cannot be wholly different; and the failure of poor films is often precisely in exaggeration, and in the intrusion of unwarranted matter owing to not perceiving where the core of the original lies' (*Letters*, 270). Exaggeration and not representing the core of the original properly are exactly the reasons why the second trilogy has been poorly accepted within Tolkien fandom.

Due to great pressure from Hollywood studios, certain elements that were introduced or emphasised in the films drastically deviate from the book, as well as from the internal logic of Tolkien's Secondary World, such as: the love triangle between Legolas, Tauriel, and Kili, which essentially compromised the attempt to bring a strong female character into the story; or utterly unrealistic barrel ride sequence; or Smaug and the molten gold scene.[17] Many respondents considered such changes to be a consequence of the desire to make the films more commercial, which led to a failure to believably represent Tolkien's imaginary world. As Tolkien himself noted, if details are to be added, 'they should at least fit the world described' (*Letters*, 272).

---

17. Carolyn Michelle, and others, pp. 207–209.

The efforts to connect the trilogies were not managed subtly, and all the references to the first trilogy combined with numerous needless additions ultimately distract the audience from the main story – the quest of the thirteen Dwarves and Bilbo to reclaim Erebor. As the research of Carolyn Michelle and others has shown, with each successive film, 'an established franchise progressively disillusioned and even alienated a significant portion of its large and enthusiastic pre-existing fan base.'[18] The alterations and exaggerations in the portrayal of events and characters (e.g. Thorin, Thranduil, Radagast) as well as the 'attributes intended to increase the trilogy's appeal to mainstream moviegoers – including the numerous action sequences, advanced computer-generated visual effects, a decidedly un-Tolkienish love triangle and the expansion of the story over three films – undermined deep engagement with the narrative storyworld'[19] and disappointed numerous members of Tolkien fandom, as demonstrated in almost all the comments above.

After gaining an insight into general attitudes about the adaptations and some major changes introduced, the question is how do they affect people's remembering of Tolkien's stories and their details? Misremembering happens in different areas of Tolkien reception; a good example is a photo of gardener Clarence Elliott which has been widely circulated as a photo of Tolkien.[20] Another one is the verse 'Not all those who

18. Ibid, p. 195.

19. Ibid, p. 12.

20. For this example and some other cases of misquoting or misappropriating Tolkien, see the Tolkienist's blog, where Marcel Aubron-Bülles has published a series of posts under the title *Things J.R.R. Tolkien has never said, done, written or had anything to do with*: https://thetolkienist.com/category/quotes/.

wander are lost', frequently encountered on the Internet in its impoverished form, without the word *those*. Some other quotes have also been mistakenly attributed to Tolkien over the years, but the greatest impact on the practice of quoting or misquoting has certainly been that of Jackson's films.

Film quotes are widely attributed to Tolkien on the Internet, some of them come from the book, but are slightly changed, e.g. Gandalf's quote 'All we have to decide is what to do with the time that is given us' which ends with 'to us' in the films and is later changed into a more personal message 'All you have to decide is what to do with the time that is given to you' in Frodo's recollection at the end of *The Fellowship of the Ring*. Some misquotations or misattributions are easier to spot, since the quotes are not from the books at all, such as Galadriel's quote 'Even the smallest person can change the course of the future'. However, if you search for it via Google, you will see that this quote is attributed to Tolkien on countless websites, leading people astray, especially if they cannot recall if it is a book quotation or not.[21] In addition to being widely circulated on the Internet, all three quotes mentioned so far have been a common motif for various forms of merchandise inspired by *The Lord of the Rings*, which prolongs their misattribution, knowingly or unknowingly.

A number of short, memorable quotes became popular due to the films; they are frequently used in the creation of memes or similar creative and intertextual fan practices, also regularly found on merchandise, but rarely misattributed, e.g., film quotes like Boromir's 'One does not simply walk

21.https://www.reddit.com/r/tolkienfans/comments/2lsiyz/is_this_galadriel_quote_in_the_book/

into Mordor.'; Pippin's 'We had one, yes. What about second breakfast?'; or Uglúk's 'Looks like meat's back on the menu, boys!'; Gandalf's film quotes 'A wizard is never late, Frodo Baggins. Nor is he early; he arrives precisely when he means to.', slightly modified book quotes 'Keep it secret, keep it safe.' and 'You shall not pass!', or the accurate ones like 'Fool of a Took!' and 'Fly, you fools!', etc. Entire speeches are also popular, like Sam's speech in Osgiliath, partially based on the book (*TT*, II, viii), but ending with a part which gets misattributed to Tolkien 'That there's some good in this world, Mr. Frodo. And it's worth fighting for.'[22] Another similar example of misattribution is Aragorn's speech at the Black Gate, for which some people honestly believe it comes from the books.[23] It is logical to assume that there are similar examples of film memories overriding the original knowledge of the books when it comes to quotes, and investigating them in detail will be in the focus of my future research.

At this point, I would like to propose a thesis that in terms of individual memory accurate adaptations are more 'dangerous' than less accurate ones, since it is easier to overlook some changes and differences when an adaptation remains faithful to 'the spirit of the original'. That is because our minds generally focus on remembering the narrative and the overall 'meaning' of the story, not so much the details, many of which are

---

22. *The Lord of the Rings: The Two Towers*, extended edition, dir. by Peter Jackson (New Line Cinema, 2002), 03:21:44 – 03:23:47.

23. I am grateful to Shaun Gunner for pointing this out in a conversation. An illustrative example of misattribution of Aragorn's speech at the Black Gate to Tolkien can be found on a popular website *Goodreads*: https://www.goodreads.com/quotes/7375724-hold-your-ground-gold-your-ground-sons-of-gondor-of

inevitably forgotten. Hence, as noted before, many people do not mind a number of changes as long as they do not deviate drastically from the core of the story.

The knowledge and memory of details are acquired through repetition, and that applies to adaptations as well as to works that inspired them, so what remains in individuals' memory is changing with each rereading of the books or rewatching of the films. The fact that the adaptations of *The Hobbit* are less accurate and faithful to the original made them less popular, but at the same time less dangerous in terms of misremembering the details of the story – people are more sensitive to changes and consequently pay more attention to them. Furthermore, *The Hobbit* trilogy was less successful in cinemas from the start, and rather than expanding it was losing its audience with each consecutive film. This is reflected in less frequent rewatchings of the films, which makes the events, characters and the quotes from them less memorable by default, 'particularly when assessed against the high standards of cinematic excellence and emotional resonance' achieved with the first trilogy.[24] As one of the respondents pointed out, the fact that *The Hobbit* films are not nearly as good as *The Lord of the Rings* trilogy makes it 'easier to ignore the claimed relation' with the original (comment no. 7 above).

It seems that the more accurate, successful, and popular an adaptation is, it becomes more seductive and able to affect our overall memory of the books. Thus, fidelity claims have a fairly contradictory nature in terms of preserving memory of the books – a faithful adaptation is more appealing to the knowing audiences for presenting the source material accurately, but

---

24. Carolyn Michelle, and others, pp. 9–12.

precisely for that reason it has a higher potential to replace the original memory of the books. For those who can swear that they remember Aragorn's speech at the Black Gate from the book, that speech fits in perfectly with the rest of the original story and they find it hard to believe that it is not a part of it. This sort of blending between *The Lord of the Rings* book and films was noted by some participants, whose memories and visions of Middle-earth and its characters have been equally shaped by both media.

In addition to affecting our memory of a story and its details, film adaptations are able to significantly alter our memories and imagination when it comes to visualising a fictional world. Hence, the influence of film images on our memory and imagination has been, besides fidelity, the second-most commonly discussed topic concerning literature-to-film adaptations, and the one participants in my research most frequently mentioned.

Visualising Middle-earth

When writing about Jackson's films, Christina Scull and Wayne Hammond remarked that it is impossible to determine if those who read the books after seeing the films were able to divorce their mental pictures from the adaptations.[25] In his analysis of the occurrence of the term 'visualisation' in fan responses from *The Lord of the Rings World Audiences* project, Martin Barker explored the ideas of 'mental imaging', pointing that such mental processes frequently involve interaction of sound,

25. Christina Scull, Wayne G. Hammond., *The J.R.R. Tolkien Companion and Guide. Reader's Guide. Part 1* (London: HarperCollinsPublishers, 2017), p. 25. Further references to this edition are given in parentheses.

touch, smell, memories, and other forms not strictly confined to images (Barker, 8, 14). He focused on Jackson's adaptations as a positive influence recognised by motivated respondents as helpful in achieving desired level of visualisation, enjoying someone else's interpretation, and having a shared vision to compare with a personal one (Barker, 18–20). The answers which regarded the films' influence on respondents' visualisation as negative were not analysed, thus not elaborating on a common stance that film imagery effaces individual visions of a fictional world created while reading. My own surveys have demonstrated a great variety of ways people relate to visual aspect of the films, ranging from avoiding seeing the films in order to escape their possible influence, to giving them credit for perfectly embodying those participants' personal visions of Middle-earth and exceeding their expectations.

In all my surveys participants were asked to determine major influences on their imagining of Middle-earth. The summary results for all 3,115 participants given in Chart 2[26] (overleaf) show that *descriptions and maps from the books* were chosen by more than 80% of the respondents and ranked first, but were closely followed by *Peter Jackson's films*. The third and fourth place were occupied by *artworks* and *book illustrations*, which

26. The categories marked with asterisk (*) in this chart were not offered as a choice in the first three surveys conducted (a total of 2,255 participants) and although they were added by some participants, the statistics would be higher if they were offered as default answers. This can be assumed based on the two later surveys (a total of 829 participants) which offered said options within this question, and where *Tolkien's illustrations* were chosen by 50.2% of the participants, *My own imagination* by 43.8% and *Music* by 12.5%. Thus, the overall results were adjusted in order to gain a more realistic insight. 500 participants were added for *Tolkien's illustrations* and *My own imagination*, and 250 participants for Music.

Chart 2. The way you imagine Middle-earth and its inhabitants is predominantly influenced by:

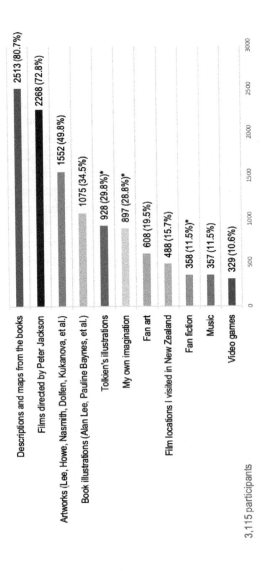

3,115 participants

is significant if we bear in mind that the art of prominent book illustrators Alan Lee and John Howe largely determined the aesthetics of the films as well.

The statistics presented indicates that visual media do make a lasting impression on our mental images of Tolkien's fictional world. As mentioned above, many concerns around adaptations are caused by the idea that visual media are able to take over our imagination and override the influence of the text, and such an attitude was present in a number of answers, several participants stating that they have deliberately avoided seeing the films in order to preserve their own vision of the world unchanged. A significant number of participants pointed out the pervasive impact the Jackson's films have had on their imagination, and whilst some of them had no problem with it, the others regretted it. The strong visual impact was described as involuntary and difficult to escape from by many of them:

> In a way I feel sometimes sad that my original childhood image of Middle-earth based on books is nowadays forgotten and pretty much replaced by the scenery from PJ films. On the other hand, and luckily, those film images are mostly accurate, beautiful, well thought of and acceptable. So I can live with them since there is no escaping. (KB, 56–60, Finland)

Some respondents expressed particular satisfaction that their own vision of Tolkien's world, formed prior to the appearance of the films and mainly influenced by the books, has been preserved despite seeing the films. In a similar vein, some participants said that their imagination rarely draws upon film imagery when reading the books, that they are able to separate them, and imagine and enjoy them as two different media telling the same story. Others pointed out that they imagine landscapes and places of Middle-earth based on the films or places they visited, but that they imagine characters based on their descriptions from the books. Some acknowledged the films' impact, but also detected subsequent influences such as games (LOTRO), rereading of the books or reading of *The Silmarillion* and other works by Tolkien. A number of participants replied that they build their personal complex visions of the world by simultaneously relying on the books, their preferred interpretations in other media, and their personal experiences; many respondents seemed to be well aware that they create a composite reconstruction of Tolkien's world in their minds based on different sources, which is aptly demonstrated by answers akin to this one: 'I very much pick and choose which aspects from all these things I agree or disagree with, but have a little of everything in my imaginations.' (Participant no. 1835, 21–25, UK) This manner of experiencing the story through different media and comparing various interpretations in order to build a personal one brings us back to one of the main reasons we enjoy adaptations – the pleasure in comparisons and oscillation between works, in some cases quite literally:

> I have to admit that film adaptations have influenced my visualisation. I even used to read the book and watch the films at the same time – I would read fifty pages, and then I would watch the film for ten minutes. Thus, I visualised the characters during reading. (Ivan Drajzl, 44, Serbia)

The decision to include Alan Lee and John Howe as concept artists for the films enabled Jackson to use their previously created and well-known imagery, which has to a large extent shaped the way people imagined and visualised Middle-earth before the films. Their involvement in the making of the films affirmed their aesthetics as a dominant influence many participants mentioned:

1.   Films left a very strong visual impact from which is now very difficult to escape. But it should be noted that the illustrators and designers working on the films largely based their vision on the original Tolkien's illustrations and illustrations by Alan Lee and John Howe, which actually makes the films very close to Tolkien's vision (at least in theory). (B.Č., 36, Serbia)

2.   I have my own visions of Middle-earth from reading the books, however due to Peter Jackson's movies I had an overload of images from Alan Lee and John Howe in my minds eye, I was fortunate to have read the books before seeing the movies. (Participant no. 1080, Netherlands)

3.   Alan Lee's illustrations were my first visual experience of Middle-earth (he illustrated my first copies of both The Hobbit and LOTR), and as he was a main concept artist for the films they ended up reflecting my existing imagination to a large degree - I was pleasantly surprised when most of The Two Towers and The Return of the King, which I read before the films came out, matched my imagination closely. (Tas Cooper, 29, UK)

As noted above and demonstrated by a sheer variety of responses, it is impossible to determine to what extent people are able or willing to divorce their mental pictures from the films, as it is a highly individual process involving personal taste, abilities, and investment. For many people, the films are a welcome supplement in their interaction with the books. Some of them explicitly stated that they 'don't have a very visual imagination' or that the films have helped them visualise

Middle-earth which was difficult for them. Others who said that the adaptations enhanced their visualisation felt it necessary to point out that the films have not completely taken over their imagination, showing their awareness of similar accusations on the account of film as a medium. A number of respondents considered their mental images formed prior to the films to be a much stronger influence, while the ones who watched the films first clearly had no problem with acknowledging their influence, since it made them interested in reading the books and exploring interpretations in other media, adding many new components to the way they understand and imagine Middle-earth. Many expressed undivided admiration for the efforts and skills invested into creating an impressive and immersive cinematic experience, praising the appearance of landscapes, architecture, and artifacts displayed in the films.

The processes of remembering and recollection are complex and multi-layered, and our memories are subjective and highly selective reconstructions; they also change over time, being 'written' anew with each repeated reading of the books or viewing of the films. Considering the close connection between imagination and memory, the ways people imagine Tolkien's world (Chart 2) testify to the main influences on their memory too, confirming that the books hold primacy despite being closely followed by the films and other visual media. Although we can agree that visual media and film images are extremely powerful and can exert an involuntary influence on memory, the opinions participants expressed demonstrated that it would be an oversimplification to claim that the films affect everyone in the same manner, overriding the original imaginings and memory of the books and replacing individual visions of Tolkien's fictional world with the vision offered by Peter Jackson and his team. Numerous media shape our thinking, interpreting, and remembering, sometimes in ways of which we are not even aware, but they certainly do so in distinctive ways and to a variable degree depending on our individual abilities, experiences, tastes, and habits, moreover, they usually work together to provide a mnemonic support for our imaginations.

Fandom and Memory

Fans have been immensely important in popularising Tolkien's fictional world from very early on and responsible for many forms of establishing and maintaining Tolkien-related memory culture, which can be sorted into the following groups:

1. institutions and organisations (e.g. Tolkien Estate, Tolkien Society, academia, fan groups);
2. memorials, monuments and other places of memory (e.g. Tolkien's grave, the Blue Plaques, Tolkien Bench and Two Trees at Oxford University Parks);
3. celebrations and rituals (e.g. Tolkien Birthday Toast, Tolkien Reading Day, Enyalië);
4. fan conventions and similar events (e.g. Oxonmoot, Mythcon, Tolkienmoot, Tolkien Thing);
5. collecting activities;
6. interpretations and adaptations in different media (text, visual arts, music, radio, theatre, comics, animation, film, games, etc.);
7. contemporary internet culture (social media, online discussion groups, forums, blogs, etc.). Thus, fandom lies at the threshold between communicative and cultural memory, in many ways resting upon informal, voluntary transmission of

memory, but also capable to formalise it in structures which can outlast individual and generational memory.

The presence of any work of art in active social memory is first and foremost a matter of reception.[27] Books that are not read and films that are not watched do not have any effect on memory. The active role of audiences in appropriating them defines the frameworks of their reception and conditions of remembrance. Hence, 'fans are increasingly becoming recognized in their role as historians, curators of material and spokespeople for generational memory' (Duffett, 409). They preserve and remember things which matter to them, and their emotional response and investment emerges as a crucial component of their drive to discover, learn, imagine, invent, create, discuss, and share the works they love with others.

This sharing and communication have been drastically changed by online interaction. The memory of any society relies on available media and technologies of communication, and new media technologies have enabled storage and dissemination of data on a scale never seen before. The Internet has become the primary communication space for fans, enabling instant social connections among individuals from different parts of the world, as well as content sharing on a global scale. It has made it easier to access information, find like-minded individuals, build a common ground, reinforce norms, share knowledge and expertise of particular texts, it provided online spaces where questions are asked, dilemmas solved, debates initiated, values and ideas questioned and negotiated. Being

---

27. Astrid Erll, *Memory in Culture* (London: Palgrave Macmillan, 2011), p. 160. Further references to this edition are given in parentheses.

a part of any fandom community is not always an easy or pleasant experience, especially if an individual wants to share or discuss opinions which do not fit into a dominant discourse within said community. In order to belong, an individual is usually expected to stick to the 'canon' – in fandoms 'issues of memory are often expressed through arguments over "canon": in other words which elements of a particular storyworld are "genuine" or "authentic" and which are non-canon' (Harvey, 3). Due to the changes in communication brought about by the Internet, contemporary fan cultures seem more open to negotiations of meaning. Although they usually favour particular ways of interpreting a text, they are also dynamic; although they strive towards a consensus, they stimulate new interpretations and offer constant opportunities for their comparison. Debates which engender new interpretations and perspectives are desirable in the context of remembering – paradoxically, reaching a consensus can lead to forgetting, while constant negotiation of meanings keeps Tolkien's works alive and continuously present in collective memory. Evaluating adaptations is a part of that process, so we could say that their sheer existence is by default contributing to it.

In addition to providing access to collective knowledge, intelligence, and experience through digital archives and social interaction, the Internet has brought about new models of cultural production. Tolkien's world has inspired numerous interpretations and adaptations of varying quality since the 1960s, in writing, music, radio, theatre, visual arts, animation, film, games, comics, etc., and this process has intensified during the last two decades, owing to increased participation opportunities provided by the Internet and digital technologies, combined with the popularity of multi-award winning film adaptations (Scull & Hammond, 8-27, 393-394). As a consequence, the field of canonical and non-canonical readings has become vast indeed, incorporating numerous creative interpretations and appropriations such as fan fiction, fan art, fan films, games, cosplay, etc. We have witnessed a surge of more or less innovative fan productivity in various media, with a varying degree of fidelity to Tolkien's works or adherence to the inner logic of his Secondary World. Simultaneously, digital technologies have altered the behaviour of experiencing imaginary worlds, causing users to move across various media platforms, and follow stories from one medium to another, striving to more fully experience their favourite fictions through all sources available.[28] As some participants stated, they rely on various sources and have 'a little of everything' in their imaginations when reconstructing Tolkien's fictional world.

The internet activities of Tolkien fans are remarkably diverse, starting from writing content on websites and blogs, participating in discussion groups, asking for advice, sharing personal opinions or scholarly research, displaying private collections of books and other Tolkien-related material, exploring, making or sharing fan art, music or fan films, writing and reading fan fiction, creating film edits, parodies, memes, etc. Individuals are largely responsible for building up the success of a certain product through their voluntary activities on social networks, such as liking, sharing, commenting, remixing, creating video explanations, parodies, memes, etc. Due to their attachment to Tolkien's works, fans are strongly

---

28. Henry Jenkins, *Convergence Culture: Where Old and New Media Collide* (New York – London: New York University Press, 2006), pp. 20-21, 97-99, 116, 120-122.

motivated to produce and circulate media materials, and their activities are best described as *memory-based making*, since they derive their significance from appealing to the specialised knowledge of fan audience, clearly dependent upon memory. Fans appropriate quotes, images, songs, video clips, and use them as the basis for their own creations which represent the forms of commenting on the original, the prior knowledge of the original being necessary for their understanding.

The impact of Jackson's films cannot be overstated in terms of digital circulation of images and quotes, e.g., almost all the existing *The Lord of the Rings* and *The Hobbit* memes exclusively rely on the films as source material. Numerous parodies, fan films, pieces of fan art, fan fiction, and music draw heavily upon the films. However, Tolkien's legendarium is much broader than *The Lord of the Rings* and *The Hobbit* and many creators are inspired by other texts or want to offer their own interpretations independent of the film adaptations. The predominance of film images can be limiting for creators' imagination, but the Internet offers plenty of other sources to be inspired with, and also a space to share different visions.

Tolkien fandom today is a global networked community based on intense affection towards Tolkien's stories, comprised of enthusiasts who invest their time and efforts in data gathering, preservation, and dissemination, the main motive behind all that activity being to honour, understand, and preserve said stories and the memory of their author. The community has its own mechanisms of identifying and dealing with the cases of misremembering, misrepresenting, or misinterpreting Tolkien, and all the attempts of using or adapting his works go through a severe scrutiny, which is adequately illustrated by now less fervent, but in many instances still ongoing debates and disagreements over Jackson's adaptations. So, although individual memories can be affected by adaptations, they also tend to be shaped and adjusted by the group, with shared elaboration being more efficient in discovering potential misrememberings. The fallibility of individual memory is corrected and made up for by collective efforts and knowledge provided by the community of fans who pool what they know in order to enhance the overall understanding of their favourite fictional world.

Canon Battles Revisited

Battles over canon are battles over memory, no matter if they are about establishing interpretative canons within fandom or academic and cultural norms which single out certain works as canonical pieces of art and literature. Aleida Assmann explains that the term canon is best used to describe 'actively circulated memory that keeps the past present'.[29] Only selected works of art become a part of that past after they have acquired a special status through the process of canonisation:

> The active dimension of cultural memory supports a collective identity and is defined by a notorious shortage of space. It is built on a small number of normative and formative texts, places, persons, artifacts, and myths which are meant to be actively circulated and communicated in ever-new presentations and performances. The working memory

29. Aleida Assmann, 'Canon and Archive', in *Cultural Memory Studies: An International and Interdisciplinary Handbook*, ed. by Astrid Erll and Ansgar Nünning (Berlin – New York: Walter de Gruyter, 2008), 97–107 (p. 98). Further references to this text are given in parentheses.

stores and reproduces the cultural capital of a society that is continuously recycled and re-affirmed. Whatever has made it into the active cultural memory has passed rigorous processes of selection, which secure for certain artifacts a lasting place in the cultural working memory of a society. This process is called canonization. (A. Assmann, 100)

Thus, a canon proscribes the works of art and literature which are constantly kept in society's active memory through educational and cultural institutions, and 'It is only a tiny segment of the vast history of the arts that has the privilege of repeated presentation and reception which ensures its aura and supports its canonical status.' (A. Assmann, 101)

'Canon formation and the writing of literary history are central mechanisms on the basis of which the 'memory of literature' is upheld in societies.' (Erll, 75) Popular works of art and literature struggle to reach the status of 'high' art which gives them a privileged place in collective memory. In order to achieve that, they usually have to remain popular for a long time, durability of their popularity making the canon-makers pay more attention to them and re-asses their value. In 2002 Jane Chance remarked that she was glad to 'see that the popular has become the canon' alluding to a growing interest and different scholarly attitudes towards Tolkien at the beginning of the 21st century, and his works finally becoming the subject of numerous academic courses and more mature literary criticism.[30] This remark points to a significant change in treatment of Tolkien's works, suggesting that they have succeeded in acquiring canonical status in academia and indeed

---

30. Jane Chance, 'Acknowledgements', in *Tolkien the Medievalist*, ed. by Jane Chance, (London – New York: Routledge, 2003).

'passed rigorous processes of selection', which ensures them 'a lasting place in the cultural working memory of a society', realised through educational system and cultural institutions. Central for the shaping and sustenance of cultural memory, 'canons are construed in order to last, and the history of canon formation shows that, against all odds, they quite often possess an extraordinary degree of longevity.'[31]

Although canons have a significant social and cultural relevance, being included in the official literary canon is not in itself enough to perpetuate cultural memory – canonical texts must be continuously re-appropriated and actualised by a community of remembrance, translated into communication and individual experience, used and interpreted in order to remain present in the active, working memory of a society. Without such actualisations, books are nothing but dead, stored, archived material with no real impact. As already noted, the fandom has kept Tolkien's stories actualised in functional, living memory since the 1960s, whether through reading and spreading knowledge about them or by using them as an inspiration. As Ann Rigney indicated, the canonised works of art and literature have a double nature as media of collective remembrance, namely, their 'monumentality' and their 'malleability' (Erll, 165). Their monumentality refers to their canonical status as 'literary monuments' which are persistent and omnipresent in terms of the number of their existing copies and the fact that they can be reprinted time and again. Their 'malleability' is their 'openness to appropriation by others',

---

31. Herbert Grabes, 'Cultural Memory and the Literary Canon', in *Cultural Memory Studies: An International and Interdisciplinary Handbook*, ed. by Astrid Erll and Ansgar Nünning (Berlin – New York: Walter de Gruyter, 2008), 311–319, (p. 311).

because texts continuously morph into 'other cultural products that recall, adapt, and revise them in both overt and indirect ways.'[32]

If we consider adaptations from this perspective, we may understand why they should be first and foremost regarded as *tools of remembering*. Artistic creation has an important role in the renewal and perpetuation of memory, and adaptations can keep the original work alive by 'giving it an afterlife it would never have had otherwise' (Hutcheon, 176). Memorable stories are usually told over and over again; their repeated representation and remediation (retelling in different media) tend to stabilise and solidify cultural memory (Erll, 141). By bringing numerous new fans into Tolkien fandom, Jackson's film adaptations were only useful for keeping Tolkien's heritage present in active memory. As Tom Shippey wisely pointed out, the film adaptations have been for many people *Another Road to Middle-earth*, reflected in the fact that almost the third of the participants in my research were drawn to the books after seeing the films. *The Lord of the Rings* film trilogy has brought about the existence of fandoms exclusively devoted to the films, but is also to be credited, over and above any previous adaptation, for bringing numerous new readers into Tolkien fandom worldwide. And that is of crucial importance if we look at it from the perspective of collective, and not individual memory.

For the majority of fans, Jackson and his team certainly did not aim to erase, corrupt, or parody the books, and in the case

32. Ann Rigney, 'The Dynamics of Remembrance: Texts Between Monumentality and Morphing', in *Cultural Memory Studies: An International and Interdisciplinary Handbook*, ed. by Astrid Erll and Ansgar Nünning (Berlin – New York: Walter de Gruyter, 2008), 345–353 (p. 349).

of the first trilogy they did their best to preserve and depict the story with fidelity, whilst taking into account the complexity of Tolkien's world, the nature of film as a medium, and some contemporary values and sensibilities. Thus, the first trilogy represents a well-balanced attempt to be faithful to the original story as much as possible whilst making it accessible for all audiences, knowing and unknowing. *The Hobbit* trilogy is more problematic in this context, and we have seen that the failure to understand the importance of conformity to the spirit of the books and adherence to the inner logic of the storyworld decreases the adaptations' chances of becoming memory making material.

The importance of the films' popularity for general remembering of Tolkien's stories was remarked upon in Chad's observation about unknowing audiences: 'when there are differences between the adaptation & original, frequently the (more popular) adaptation becomes considered canon by non-readers' (Chad Bornholdt, USA, 47), emphasising the fact that some people who have encountered Tolkien's storyworld only through the films think that they 'know Tolkien', to a huge dismay of book-lovers. Nevertheless, Tolkien's fictional world has been a part of the public imaginary for several decades before the films, the popularity of books and their cult status are not jeopardised by the adaptations' popularity or the existence of fandoms devoted to them. The films introduced new possibilities of experiencing Tolkien's imaginary world, extended its reach and boosted its popularity. Hence, academic canonisation of Tolkien coupled with his ever-growing popularity are strong indicators that his legacy is safe and remarkably 'far from passing into the "merciful oblivion" predicted by Philip Toynbee' (Shippey, 365).

So, is adapting Tolkien (mis)remembering Tolkien? We have seen that the process of adapting necessarily involves adapters' decisions to remember with fidelity or knowingly misremember some elements to suit their creative aims, and that some changes are inevitable when translating a story into different medium and trying to make it relevant for contemporary audiences. The ambiguous relation towards adaptations is caused by the interplay of innovation, recognition, and remembrance inherent in the adaptation process combined with the fear that a successful adaptation could replace the memory of the books. Adaptations are more likely to produce a pleasurable viewing if they are aligned with peoples' memory of the books and drastic deviations from it are described as 'spoiling' and 'misremembering' the source text. However, their accuracy and fidelity to the original can have the opposite effect and actually increase their potential to take the place of the books as memory making material and a favoured version of the story. We have seen that many fans expressed concerns about the films' influence on their imagination, labelling it 'difficult to escape from'. Nonetheless, the films overriding the knowledge of the books and affecting people's remembering of the story do so more frequently in cases when the films have become the dominant manner of experiencing the story: constant rewatchings of the films unaccompanied by rereadings of the books can make the memory based on adaptations outweigh the one formed in the course of reading. Individual memory is transmedial, determined by multiple sources, and shaped by our habits, cultural background, value systems, knowledge, mental abilities, personal taste and interests, but also by collective frameworks of memory. Misremembering caused by the adaptations is corrected by the activities of fan community, where group knowledge and discussions balance the subjective visions, and all potential misinterpretations get scrutinised in the process of canon formation and negotiation. Combined with official legal organisations like the Tolkien Estate or Middle-earth Enterprises and numerous institutions and scholars involved in research and preservation of Tolkien's legacy, the fandom has a crucial role in the shaping of contemporary communicative and cultural memory related to the Professor and his works. His fictional world gains additional value and significance through increased use, and new interpretations, appropriations, and adaptations can motivate discussions and attract new people, thus reinforcing the presence of Tolkien's heritage in active social memory. In this context, Peter Jackson's film adaptations have been extremely beneficial, and their positive impact surpasses the negative one. Adapting Tolkien can mean both remembering and misremembering Tolkien, but certainly not forgetting, and no interpretation, however popular, can really harm his legacy.

References

Assmann, Aleida, 'Canon and Archive', in *Cultural Memory Studies: An International and Interdisciplinary Handbook*, ed. by Astrid Erll and Ansgar Nünning (Berlin – New York: Walter de Gruyter, 2008), pp. 97–107.

Assmann, Jan, 'Communicative and Cultural Memory', in *Cultural Memory Studies: An International and Interdisciplinary Handbook*, ed. by Astrid Erll and Ansgar Nünning (Berlin – New York: Walter de Gruyter, 2008), pp. 109–118.

Barker, Martin, 'Envisaging "Visualisation": Some challenges from the international *Lord of the Rings project*', *Film–Philosophy*, v. 10, n. 3 (2006), pp. 1–25.

Chance, Jane, 'Acknowledgements', in *Tolkien the Medievalist*, ed. by Jane Chance, (London – New York: Routledge, 2003).

Duffett, Mark, *Understanding Fandom. An Introduction to the Study of Media Fan Culture* (New York – London: Bloomsbury, 2013).

Elliott, Kamilla, *Theorizing Adaptation* (New York: Oxford University Press, 2020).

Ellis, John, 'The Literary Adaptation', *Screen*, Vol. 23.1 (May/June 1982), pp. 3–5.

Erll, Astrid, *Memory in Culture* (London: Palgrave Macmillan, 2011).

Grabes, Herbert, 'Cultural Memory and the Literary Canon', in *Cultural Memory Studies: An International and Interdisciplinary Handbook*, ed. by Astrid Erll and Ansgar Nünning (Berlin – New York: Walter de Gruyter, 2008), pp. 311–319.

Harvey, Colin B., *Fantastic Transmedia. Narrative, Play and Memory Across Science Fiction and Fantasy Storyworlds* (London: Palgrave Macmillan, 2015).

Hutcheon, Linda, with Siobhan O'Flynn, *A Theory of Adaptation*, 2nd ed. (London and New York: Routledge, 2013).

Jenkins, Henry, *Textual Poachers: Television Fans and Participatory Culture* (London – New York: Routledge, 1992).
—— *Convergence Culture: Where Old and New Media Collide* (New York – London: New York University Press, 2006).

Krauss, Rosalind, *The Originality of the Avant-Garde and Other Modernist Myths* (Cambridge, MA – London: The MIT Press, 1986).

Lee, Rensselaer W., 'Ut Pictura Poesis: The Humanistic Theory of Painting', *The Art Bulletin*, Vol. 22, No. 4 (Dec., 1940), pp. 197–269.

Michelle, Carolyn, and others, *Fans, Blockbusterisation, and the Transformation of Cinematic Desire: Global Receptions of the Hobbit Film Trilogy* (London: Palgrave Macmillan, 2017).

Mitchell, W. J. T., *What Do Pictures Want. The Lives and Loves of Images* (Chicago and London: The University of Chicago Press, 2005).

Rigney, Ann, 'The Dynamics of Remembrance: Texts Between Monumentality and Morphing', in *Cultural Memory Studies: An International and Interdisciplinary Handbook*, ed. by Astrid Erll and Ansgar Nünning (Berlin – New York: Walter de Gruyter, 2008), pp. 345–353.

Ross, Lee, David Greene, Pamela House, 'The "False Consensus Effect": An Egocentric Bias in Social Perception and Attribution Processes', *Journal of Experimental Social Psychology*, 13.3 (May 1977), pp. 279–301.

Scull, Christina, and Hammond, Wayne G., *The J.R.R. Tolkien Companion and Guide. Reader's Guide. Part 1* (London: HarperCollins, 2017).

Shippey, Tom, 'Another Road to Middle-earth: Jackson's Movie Trilogy', *Roots and Branches: Selected Papers on Tolkien* by Tom Shippey, ed. by Thomas Honegger (Zurich: Walking Tree Publishers, 2007), pp. 365–386.

Tolkien, J.R.R., *The Letters of J.R.R. Tolkien* ed. by Humphrey Carpenter (Boston – New York: Houghton Mifflin Harcourt, 2000).

—— *The Lord of the Rings* (London: HarperCollinsPublishers, 2014).

—— *The Lord of the Rings: The Two Towers*, extended edition, dir. by Peter Jackson (New Line Cinema, 2002).

Adapting Tolkien Beyond Arda, or, How to Navigate the Political Minefield of the International Astronomical Union in Order to Name Features on Titan, Pluto, and Charon After Middle-earth

Kristine Larsen

Introduction

Names were important to Tolkien. From his famous appropriation of *earendel* from Cynewulf's *Crist* (*Letters*, 414) to his continued agonizing for a consistent meaning for the root **ros* in Elros (*Peoples*, 367), Turin's ironic self-designation as Turambar –"Master of Doom" – (*Silmarillion*, 352), and Aragorn's childhood name of Estel – "Hope" – (*RK*, Appendix A, I, v), for Tolkien names were not things to be taken lightly. There are mythical, philological, cultural, and even political considerations, especially among the elves (*Morgoth*, 214-17). Tolkien's professional interest in names is apparent in a 1932 essay in which he traces the name *Nodens* (found in inscriptions in Lydney Park) to an ancient king of what is now Ireland and even further back etymologically to its Indo-European roots (Tolkien, 'Nodens', 182). Indeed, in a 1971 BBC radio interview Tolkien offered 'It gives me great pleasure, a good name' (Dickerson and Evans, 7).

As I have described elsewhere, scientists from numerous disciplines (including paleontology, entomology, geology, and astronomy) have paid homage to their favorite author and his subcreated mythology by naming discoveries after characters and places in Middle-earth, and even the author himself (Larsen, 'SAURON', 223). In the realm of astronomy, these include the crater Tolkien on the planet Mercury, the asteroids Bilbo, Tolkien, and Sauron, and the binary trans-Neptunian Kuiper Belt objects Manwë/Thorondor and Varda/Ilmarë (Park and Chamberlin).

Despite the existence of commercial enterprises promising to name a star after a loved one, the official task of designating all features beyond earth falls to the International Astronomical Union (IAU). In spite of the strictly scientific nature of the organization, the process has historically been fraught with politics. It is therefore not a trivial task for scientists to honor the works of Tolkien by adapting names from Middle-earth to features on worlds elsewhere in our solar system. Mythology and philology are frequently involved (something that would have pleased Tolkien). This essay summarizes several successes and two ongoing attempts to name features on other worlds in honor of Middle-earth.

Politics of astronomical naming and the IAU

Prior to 1919 there was no international standardization of many astronomical names, including the constellations and features on Mars and the Moon. In response to this increasingly problematic situation, the International Astronomical Union was created in the wake of the Versailles Treaty. Its self-stated mission is to 'promote and safeguard the science of astronomy in all its aspects, including research, communication, education and development, through international cooperation' (IAU, 'About'). The IAU currently has over 10,000 individual active members in 107 countries, with 82 countries listed as National Members. Its activities include the organization of international meetings and 'unambiguous astronomical nomenclature', boasting that 'the IAU serves as the internationally recognized authority for assigning designations to celestial bodies and surface features on them' (IAU, 'About'). However, past IAU General Secretary Thierry Montmerle admits that

> the role of the IAU in designations [...] or nomenclature [...] was never made official by an international political organization (like the League of Nations or the United Nations) [...] [but] I personally believe that the role of the IAU in naming celestial objects [...] is de facto sanctioned every three years at the GA [General Assembly] by the votes of its National representatives. (Montmerle, 92).

One of the first highly political debates the IAU arbitrated was the assignment of names for features on the far side of the Moon in the 1960s in response to the first American and Soviet lunar probes (Montmerle, 91-92). But clearly the IAU's most infamous decision was the vote of the 2006 General Assembly to adopt an official definition for an astronomical planet. The decision was necessitated by two factors – a preponderance of evidence collected since its 1930 discovery that Pluto was dissimilar in numerous ways from the other eight classical planets and the discovery of an increasing number of Pluto-like bodies beyond the orbit of Neptune. In a decision that has been widely and publicly debated since, the IAU voted to adopt a definition of planet and reclassify Pluto as a dwarf planet.[1]

In contrast with the planet definition controversy, the IAU has well-established set of rules for the naming of other objects within our solar system as well as surface features on those objects. Working Groups are charged with each type of object. For example, the Working Group for Small Body Nomenclature approves a proposed name submitted by the discoverer of an asteroid or other minor planet. All names must be 16 characters or less in length (preferably a single word), 'pronounceable (in some language), non-offensive, [and] not too similar to an existing name of a Minor Planet or natural Planetary satellite' (IAU, 'Naming'). There are also restrictions concerning recent politicians and military leaders, and naming bodies after one's pet or company are problematic. It is clear that the names of the minor planets Bilbo and Tolkien meet these basic criteria.

There are additional regulations for special populations of minor planets. For example, objects in stable orbits that approach or cross the orbit of Neptune (called resonant trans-Neptunian Objects [TNOs]) but have orbital periods different from that of Neptune are 'given mythological names associated with the underworld', while objects in stable orbits beyond Neptune (called classical TNOs) are 'given mythological names associated with creation' (IAU, 'Naming'). An example of the first class is Manwë. The official citation reads 'In J.R.R. Tolkien's mythology, Manwë is foremost among the deities who rule the world. Manwë takes special responsibility for the air and winds. He resides in the Undying Lands across the

---

1. The interested reader is directed to Howard (2012), Jewitt and Luu (2007), and Messer (2010) for more details on this controversy.

western ocean from Middle Earth' (Park and Chamberlin). The mention of the 'Undying Lands' was apparently sufficient in the eyes of the IAU to justify a connection to an underworld. Compare this with the classical TNO Varda, whose citation highlights her creative powers: 'In J.R.R. Tolkien's mythology, Varda is the queen of the stars, the star-kindler. She is the deity who, prior to the birth of the first humans, created the stars and constellations. She also set the vessels of the Sun and Moon upon their appointed courses above the girdle of the Earth' (Park and Chamberlin). Names are sometimes selected due to some deep philosophical or philological connection, as in the case of the minor planet Sauron, named for 'a fictional character in J.R.R. Tolkien's fantasy novel *The Lord of the Rings*. He created the One Ring to rule the rings of power. Due to Sauron's war-like nature, a Mars-crossing minor planet was chosen to receive his name' (Park and Chamberlin). There are also general rules and conventions, for example that nomenclature should be 'simple, clear, and unambiguous', that names should reflect an international balance where possible, that names of 'military or religious significance' should be avoided. Important for our discussion here is that 'Accessible and authoritative sources, including Internet sources, are required for adopted names' (IAU, 'IAU Rules and Conventions').

While the highly detailed protocol might seem unnecessarily rigid, one very practical goal of the process is to avoid an embarrassing mistake that would necessitate a retraction, as nearly happened in the case of Arrokath/Ultima Thule. Trans-Neptunian object 2014 MU69 was originally nicknamed Ultima Thule after 'a mythical, far-northern island in medieval literature and cartography [...] beyond the borders of the known world' (Talbert). The name had been suggested by approximately 40 individuals in a naming contest and seemed mythologically consistent for the most distant object slated to be visited by a human-made spacecraft, the New Horizons spacecraft, after its Pluto encounter. Unfortunately, an article by *Newsweek* pointed out that the name had previously been co-opted by Nazis and white Supremacists, leading to a firestorm of controversy (Bartels). As a result, the New Horizons team quickly suggested a replacement name for official consideration, Arrokoth, meaning 'sky' in the tongue of the indigenous Powhatan tribe of Maryland, home to the mission. Mission scientist Simon Porter admitted of the kerfuffle 'Basically, not enough due diligence was done' (Ahmed).

Central to such 'due diligence' should be reliance on a trustworthy reference for the etymology and mythology of the proposed names. Indeed, the IAU website's 'Feature Name Request' form notes that it '*is preferable to use a source that is already established in the gazetteer*'. However, in the case of Tolkien-related names it is apparent how potential problems could arise, given that there are currently only two Tolkien-related sources in the gazetteer: Robert Foster's 1978 *The Complete Guide to Middle-earth* and *The Fellowship of the Ring*. Indeed, there is currently only a single example where the latter is cited as the authoritative source, the naming of a boulder on the minor planet Bennu as Thorondor Saxum: 'King of the Eagles in the Middle-earth, the fictional setting in fantasy novels by English author J.R.R. Tolkien, the greatest of all eagles, with a wingspan of 55m (approximately as this boulder)' (IAU, 'Thorondor Saxum').

The naming of this boulder reflects a final yet vitally important piece of the IAU naming conventions – the surface features of each world follow a specific set of conventions or themes. In the case of the minor planet Bennu, named after an Egyptian deity depicted as a heron, all features are named for birds and bird-like creatures. Craters on Mercury are named for famous authors, artists, and musicians, with Tolkien's namesake crater lying close to the planet's north pole. Another example is that (nearly all) features on the planet Venus are named after women. However, the IAU's reliance on secondary and tertiary sources for the verification of names has led them to violate their own rules in the case of several Venusian features. Six features on Venus are named after the same Tibetan Buddhist deity (just different manifestations), while another should have been disqualified on political/religious grounds (Larsen, 'Prostrate', 195). It is therefore important to stress that the authoritative source for nearly all Tolkien related names (as far as the IAU is concerned) is Foster's 1978 volume, clearly a secondary source of information.

Titan and the 'Lord of the Rings'

As a gas giant planet, Saturn has no solid surface and hence no named features. Each of its major moons has a unique naming scheme; for example features on Tethys are named for characters and locations in Homer's *Odyssey* and on Enceladus for those in Burton's *Arabian Nights*. Titan, the largest moon, is only slightly smaller than the planet Mercury and plays host to numerous types of terrain; it was therefore appropriate to define separate themes by type of feature. Along with features named for planets in Frank Herbert's *Dune* series and characters from Isaac Asimov's *Foundation* series, mountains (montes) are named for mountains of Middle-earth and colles (small hills) for characters in Middle-earth. Thirteen mountains or mountain

133

ranges were approved between 2011-12, with the fourteenth – Moria Montes – added in 2015 (IAU, 'Titan'). These include Angmar Montes, Doom Mons, Erebor Mons, Misty Montes, Mithrim Montes (the tallest on Titan), and Taniquetil Montes, with the stated source for every name being Foster's volume. Lost are the subtleties of each example, each bearing the same origin statement – 'Name of a mountain from Middle-earth, the fictional setting in fantasy novels by J.R.R. Tolkien', with the exception of Moria Montes, which offers 'Name of three massive peaks, the Mountains of Moria, at the midpoint of the Misty Mountains range from Middle-earth, the fictional setting in fantasy novels by J.R.R. Tolkien' (IAU 'Titan'). The six named colles were named in two batches, with Foster's book as the authoritative reference: Arwen, Bilbo, Faramir, Handir, and Nimloth were approved in 2012 and Gandalf in 2015. A typical origin statement is Faramir's: 'Wise man of nobility; character from Middle-earth, the fictional setting in fantasy novels by J.R.R. Tolkien' (IAU, 'Titan').

In his blog *Illusory Promise*, Val Nolan attempts to draw connections between the larger Cassini mission largely responsible for mapping Titan and Tolkien's mythology. The probe's controversial plutonium powered thermoelectric generator is compared with the machinations of 'Sauroman [sic], the industrializer of green valleys with a "mind of metal and wheels"', while the choice of Arwen's name to grace hilly terrain is said to be 'in keeping with Titan nomenclature's emphasis on deities of beauty' (Nolan). Interesting Freudian slip withstanding, the only mention of 'beauty' in the Titanian classification is for fluctūs, flow terrain, which is named for deities of beauty. Nolan does make a valid point that NASA scientists have long quipped that Saturn is the true 'Lord of the Rings'. For example, as Cassini neared Saturn in 2004 JPL Director Charles Elachi offered 'Our objective is very simple -- to allow us to rewrite the story of the "Lord of the Rings"' (Maugh III). If the intention truly was to riff off Saturn as the 'Lord of the Rings', wouldn't it have made more sense to select characters more closely aligned with the Ring (such as Isildur, Boromir, or Gollum)? We do not know if these names were suggested and rejected for some reason, or if they are in the queue for approval.

Pluto and Charon

As Jewitt and Luu (135) note, there is a minority population of scientists with a vested interest in overturning the IAU's planet definition, in particular those involved with the discovery of Pluto and Pluto-sized TNOs (which would then qualify for planethood), and members of the New Horizons mission. When the unmanned probe was launched on January 19, 2006, its destination was the *ninth* planet; when it conducted its historic flyby on July 14, 2015 it changed our understanding of the now *dwarf planet* Pluto and its moons. In particular, New Horizons Principal Investigator Alan Stern has been a particularly vociferous critic of the IAU definition. For example, in 2018 Stern and co-authors used a historical survey of uses of the word *planet* in astronomical papers to argue that Pluto should never have been reclassified (Metzger et al., 21).

In the aftermath of the reclassification of Pluto, Stern had come into direct conflict with the IAU for his role in the creation of the Uwingu website, a for-profit company that raised money for educational and scientific projects between 2012-17 through an entirely unofficial public naming of planets around other stars (exoplanets) and craters on Mars, both involving a 'research crowd-funding fee' (Montmerle, 99). Comments by Uwingu co-founder Doug Griffith that called the IAU a 'self-licking ice cream cone' only added to the tension (Boyle). However it should be noted that in the wake of the tense back and forth between the two entities the IAU did solicit the input of the public in creating 'public names' (as opposed to 'scientific designations') for 260 exoplanet systems in 2013 as well as suggesting and voting on names for potential features on Pluto and its largest moon, Charon, before New Horizons arrived at the dwarf planetary system (IAU, 'Can One Buy'; IAU, 'Campaign'). For the latter campaign, all names had to follow the IAU rules for nomenclature and 'be associated with' the themes selected by the Working Group for Planetary System Nomenclature (WG-PSN). The New Horizons team was responsible for considering the suggestions and making formal recommendations to the IAU for approval (IAU, 'Campaign').

In keeping with previous planetary naming traditions, the general theme of Plutonian features plays upon the deity's classical role as god of the underworld, while secondary themes acknowledge the history of the discovery of Pluto and its moons. Charon's theme was one of exploration and voyages. As the remarkably detailed pictures streamed back from New Horizons, mission scientists found themselves buried in an embarrassment of riches in terms of the numbers and diversity of icy surface features on both bodies. Knowing that official IAU designations were years away, the New Horizons team was quick to assign informal nicknames to many of the features, at first based on shape (for example, the 'whale' and the 'heart') and then assigning them informal names that would later show up on maps and in scientific publications, necessitating the common disclaimer footnote 'All feature names used in this paper are informal' (Moore et al., 1284).[2] For example, a line of dark features or maculae on Pluto collectively dubbed 'the Brass Knuckles' were given informal names including

> Meng-Po, the goddess of forgetfulness in Chinese mythology; Balrog, a creature in J.R.R. Tolkien's 'Lord of the Rings' books; and Vucub Came and Hun Came, death gods of Mayan mythology. 'We got tired of calling it the dark spot on the left and the dark spot on the right,' said Jeffrey M. Moore, the leader of the geology, geophysics and imaging team. (Chang, 2015).

A second dark spot on Pluto received a Tolkienian nickname, Morgoth Macula.

Charon's theme of exploration and voyage became a playground for the New Horizons Team, with informal names such as Kirk, Sulu, Serenity, Nostromo, and Tardis popping up on the first maps, also with the requisite disclaimers of informality. The largest and most surprising feature on Charon was easily its dark red north polar ice cap, quickly christened Mordor Macula, and dominating both the photos released in real time by the Team and the initial map of the moon published a scant two months later (Stern et al., aad1815-3). To say that the name – informal as it was – took off would be an understatement. An Instagram post from the Obama White House the day after the New Horizons flyby celebrated a picture

---

2. For example, see http://pluto.jhuapl.edu/Galleries/Featured-Images/pdfs/Pluto-Map-Annotated.pdf

of Charon with the caption 'One does not simply fly 3 billion miles to take a photo of Mordor, the dark spot on top of Pluto's moon Charon'. An explanation for the coloration of Charon's north polar ice cap came a year later, the seasonal migration of methane from Pluto to Charon and resulting interactions with ultraviolet light (Grundy et al., 65). The best appropriation of the explanation is Phil Plait's *SyfyWire* article 'It Turns Out Methane Can Simply Walk Into Mordor.' Over the intervening years the informal names for the features of Pluto and Charon were routinely used by scientists, as they awaited formal action by the IAU.

In August 2016 (after numerous papers had been written on the findings of New Horizon at Pluto and the informal naming of many features had been introduced to the public) the WG-PSN tweaked the rules slightly (with input from the New Horizons Team) and aligned specific themes with particular types of features. For example, Pluto's faculae (bright spots), maculae (dark spots), and sulci (furrows and ridges) were assigned to 'Gods, goddesses, and other beings associated with the Underworld from mythology, folklore and literature' (Schulz) while Charon's maculae, plana (plains) and terrae (large land masses) were specified for 'Destinations and milestones of fictional space and other exploration' (Schulz). Was this revision to the nomenclature due to what former IAU General Secretary Thierry Montmerle (105) vaguely termed 'remaining frictions with the IAU, about the characterization and naming of Pluto surface features'? At any rate, while he declares the 'Pluto War' to have been ended, the point remains that nearly five years after the New Horizons flyby only a fraction of the surface features on Pluto have received official names (Montmerle, 105).

Conclusion: Whither Mordor Macula?

As of the writing of this paper, only 37 features have had their names officially adopted by the IAU on Pluto (approved in several batches between August 2017 – January 2020) and 12 on Charon (all approved on 11 April 2018). No maculae have been sanctioned on either world, so the Tolkienien names remain in limbo (IAU, 'Charon'; IAU, 'Pluto'). One might argue that the IAU is concerned with blatantly popular culture related names, as among the features still yet to be ratified are those from *Doctor Who*, *Star Trek*, *Firefly*, and other recent sci fi media. However the crater Dorothy is named for the character in *The Wizard of Oz*, Nemo is named for the Captain of the fictional Nautilus, and Pirx for a spaceship pilot in the sci-fi stories of Stanislaw Lem (IAU, 'Charon'). Montmerle (105) offers that the aforementioned 'remaining frictions' were 'not so much about the names themselves, but about the exact definition and borders of the features… drawn, as for the Moon, from geological terminology (in Latin)'. However, it is curious that defining the borders of dark areas on a brighter icy surface should be a sticking point.

From a mythological point of view we find ourselves in the curious position of acknowledging that the suggested names might not be a good fit with the IAU guidelines, as there is no clear 'Underworld' in Tolkien's legendarium (although there are mines, caves, and subterranean lairs). The closest thing would be the Halls of Mandos (in terms of a shadowy region of the dead), although recall that in the case of the TNO Manwë the reference to the Undying Lands was apparently sufficient for the IAU. If we look at the Plutonian names that have been approved, they all clearly reference an "Underworld" in their description, or are examples of pioneers of exploration or persons who contributed to our understanding of Pluto. Examples of the first group include Adlivun Cavus, the 'Underworld in Inuit myths' and Hekla Cavus, 'An Icelandic volcano believed to be the entrance to Hell in medieval European times' (IAU, 'Pluto').

Recall that the two officially approved sources of names are Foster's *The Complete Guide to Middle-earth* and *The Fellowship of the Ring*. Morgoth is problematic if one relies on these sources. Foster's brief entry does not reference his subterranean tendencies, although it does gloss the name as 'Dark Enemy of the World' (344). The entry under *Melkor* (which the IAU technically does not have to consider since it was the name *Morgoth* that is under consideration) is also less than helpful. Indeed, if one takes Foster literally without knowing much about Tolkien, the line 'he searched in the Void for the Flame Imperishable' could actually support this name as a voyager or explorer, a category for features of Charon (321). Morgoth is only named once in *The Fellowship of the Ring*, in the phrase 'a Balrog of Morgoth', a 'terror' whom Celeborn dreaded slept 'under Caradhras' (II, vii). While the Balrog was encountered in a mine and crashes – with Gandalf – into 'the abyss', it was not a realm of the dead (*FR*, II, v). Similarly Foster describes the Balrogs as 'cloaked in darkness' and notes that after the First Age they 'hid deep underground' (38-39), but does not make a clear connection with an Underworld (as in a Hadean realm of the dead). One would have to appeal to the god Pluto as the patron of mines and mining in order to make a clear case. Balrogs and Morgoth have far less connection with the Undying Lands than Manwë, especially if you use Foster as your reference.

Having failed to provide clear support for these names, what of Mordor Macula on Charon? Calli Arcale suggests that the northerly feature 'should be called Utumno, if you've read your *Silmarillion*', a curious statement as neither Mordor nor Utumno were frequently intentional travel destinations in Middle-earth (Arcale). Foster's entry is, again, less than supportive. Frodo's journey is not mentioned, and it is only a travel destination if one considers the Nazgûl, who 'entered Mordor and began the slow preparation of the land for the return of Sauron' (344). *The Fellowship of the Ring* potentially saves the day, as Elrond finally reasons, 'Now at this last we must take a hard road, a road unforeseen. There lies our hope, if hope it be. To walk into peril – to Mordor. We must send the Ring to the Fire' (II, ii). However, Frodo's was hardly a voyage of exploration.

If I were to be asked (and I assure you, I have not been), I would suggest two Tolkienian names as worthy of features on Charon: a crater for Eärendil (following the theme of 'fictional and mythological voyagers, travelers and explorers') and Vingilot Chasmata (aligned with the theme of 'fictional and mythological vessels of space and other exploration') (Schulz). While Foster's brief descriptions make only meager connections to exploration, Bilbo's poem in Rivendell 'Eärendil was a mariner' clearly speaks for itself. In addition, while Eärendil was connected with the planet Venus (the Evening Star), all features of that planet must be named after female characters, as previously noted, thus rendering him ineligible for Venusian honors.

Similarly, I would argue for the naming of a feature on Pluto for Nienna, a character with considerable connection to both the Undying Lands in general, and the Halls of Mandos (the realm of her brother) specifically. Entering the pantheon in the earliest iterations, Nienna was first introduced as the merciless death goddess Fui, whose clouds send tears and 'despairs and hopeless mourning, sorrows and blind grief' (*Lost Tales I*, 77). As Tolkien revised the legendarium throughout the next few decades, and especially during the writing of *The Lord of the Rings*, Nienna's character simultaneously softened and strengthened, reflecting the importance of mercy and pity in both Tolkien's legendarium and personal ethos (Larsen, 'Power', 207). Of course, this same argument would certainly support the naming of a resonant TNO for Nienna (an object akin to the body named in honor of Manwë).

Thierry Montmerle (90) reflects that to some in the general public '*naming* is equivalent to *owning*', a view he outright rejects. I suspect Tolkien would follow suit, insisting instead that the name belongs to the object it signifies. For as Treebeard explains to the Hobbits, 'Real names tell you the story of the things they belong to in my language' (*TT*, III, iv). The features of Pluto and Charon have so far failed to reveal their real names to us, but perhaps our Entish patience will be rewarded in the end.

Bibliography

Ahmed, Issam, 'NASA renames faraway ice world after Nazi-link backlash (Update)', 2019 <https://phys.org/news/2019-11-nasa-renames-faraway-ice-world.html> [accessed 7 August 2020].

Arcale, Calli, 'Naming the Features of Pluto and Charon, with a Sci-Fi Flair', 2015 <https://fractalwonder.wordpress.com/2015/08/02/naming-the-features-of-pluto-and-charon-with-a-sci-fi-flair/> [accessed 7 August 2020].

Bartels, Meghan, 'NASA Named its Next New Horizons Target Ultima Thule, a Mythical Land with a Nazi Connection', Newsweek, 14 March 2018 <https://www.newsweek.com/nasa-named-its-next-new-horizons-target-ultima-thule-mythical-land-nazi-844318> [accessed 7 August 2020].

Boyle, Alan, 'Mars Crater-naming Campaign Sparks an International Blowup', *NBC News*, 11 March 2014 <https://www.nbcnews.com/science/space/mars-crater-naming-campaign-sparks-international-blowup-n50271> [accessed 7 August 2020].

Carpenter, Humphrey, ed., *The Letters of J.R.R. Tolkien* (Boston: Houghton Mifflin, 2000).

Chang, Kenneth, 'NASA's New Horizons Spacecraft Sends Signal From Pluto to Earth', *New York Times*, 14 July 2015 <https://www.nytimes.com/2015/07/15/science/space/nasa-new-horizons-spacecraft-reaches-pluto.html> [accessed 7 August 2020].

Dickerson, Matthew, and Jonathan Evans, *Ents, Elves, and Eriador: The Environmental Vision of J.R.R. Tolkien* (Lexington: The University Press of Kentucky, 2011).

Foster, Robert, *The Complete Guide to Middle-earth* (New York: Ballantine Books, 1978).

Grundy, W.M. et al. 'The Formation of Charon's Red Poles From Seasonally Cold-trapped Volatiles', *Science*, 539 (2016), pp. 65-68.

143

Howard, Sethanne, 'Why Pluto is Not a Planet Anymore or How Astronomical Objects Get Names', *Journal of the Washington Academy of Sciences*, 98.4 (2012), pp. 3-14.

IAU, 'About', <https://www.iau.org/administration/about/> [accessed 7 August 2020].
—— 'Campaign for Public Participation in Naming Features on Pluto', 24 March 2015 <https://www.iau.org/news/pressreleases/detail/iau1502/> [accessed 7 August 2020].
—— 'Can One Buy the Right to Name a Planet?' 12 April 2013 <https://www.iau.org/news/pressreleases/detail/iau1301/> [accessed 7 August 2020].
—— 'Charon', <https://planetarynames.wr.usgs.gov/SearchResults?target=CHARON> [accessed 7 August 2020].
—— 'Feature Name Request', <https://planetarynames.wr.usgs.gov/FeatureNameRequest> [accessed 7 August 2020].
—— 'IAU Rules and Conventions', <https://planetarynames.wr.usgs.gov/Page/Rules> [accessed 7 August 2020].
—— 'Naming of Astronomical Objects', <https://www.iau.org/public/themes/naming/> [accessed 7 August 2020].
—— 'Pluto', <https://planetarynames.wr.usgs.gov/SearchResults?target=PLUTO> [accessed 7 August 2020].
—— 'Thorondor Saxum', Gazetteer of Planetary Nomenclature <https://planetarynames.wr.usgs.gov/Feature/15905;jsessionid=33D11CEF9B34622CD2629ABFA04FA4D6?__fsk=-393900795> [accessed 7 August 2020].
—— 'Titan', https://planetarynames.wr.usgs.gov/SearchResults?target=TITAN [accessed 7 August 2020].

Jewitt, David, and Jane X. Lu, 'Pluto, Perception and Planetary Politics', *Daedalus*, 136.1 (2007), pp. 132-36.

Larsen, Kristine, '"I Prostrate to the Goddess Foe Destroyer" - Tibetan Buddhism and the (mis)Naming of Venusian Features', *Journal of International Women's Studies*, 7.4 (2006), 186-97 <http://vc.bridgew.edu/jiws/vol7/iss4/12/>.
—— 'SAURON, Mount Doom, and Elvish Moths: The Influence of Tolkien on Modern Science', Tolkien Studies, 4 (2007), pp. 223-34.

—— 'The Power of Pity and Tears: The Evolution of Nienna in the Legendarium', in *Perilous and Fair: Women in the Works and Life of J.R.R. Tolkien*, ed. by Janet Brennan Croft and Leslie Donovan (Altadena: Mythopoeic Press, 2015), pp. 189-203.

Maugh III, Thomas H., 'Craft Poised to Run Rings Around Saturn', *Los Angeles Times*, 29 June 2004 <https://www.latimes.com/archives/la-xpm-2004-jun-29-sci-cassini29-story.html> [accessed 7 August 2020].

Messer, Lisa R. 'The Problem with Pluto: Conflicting Cosmologies and the Classification of Planets', *Social Studies of Science*, 40. 2 (2010), pp. 187-214.

Metzger, Philip T., Mark V. Sykes, Alan Stern, and Kirby Runyon, 'The reclassification of asteroids from planets to non-planets', *Icarus*, 319 (2019), pp. 21-32.

Montmerle, Thierry, 'The IAU, from New Worlds to Exoworlds: recollections of a mandate', in *Under One Sky: The IAU Centenary Symposium*, ed. by C. Sterken, J. Hearnshaw and D. Valls-Gabaud (Cambridge: Cambridge University Press, 2019), pp. 90-111.

Moore, Jeffrey M. et al., 'The geology of Pluto and Charon through the eyes of New Horizons', *Science*, 351 (2016), pp. 1284-93.

Nolan, Val, 'Tolkien on Titan: Fantasy Fiction and Solar System Nomenclature', *Illusory Promise*, 6 February 2014 <https://illusorypromise. wordpress.com/2014/06/02/tolkien-on-titan-fantasy-fiction-and-solar-system-nomenclature/> [accessed 7 August 2020].

ObamaWhiteHouse, *Instagram post on Mordor Macula*, 15 July 2015 <https://www.instagram.com/p/5LYjvFQik0/?utm_source=ig_embed> [accessed 7 August 2020].

Park, Ryan S., and Alan B. Chamberlin, 'JPL Small-Body Database Browser', <https://ssd.jpl.nasa.gov/sbdb.cgi> [accessed 7 August 2020].

Plait, Phil, 'It Turns Out Methane Can Simply Walk Into Mordor', *SyFyWire*, 1 March 2017 <https://www.syfy.com/syfywire/it-turns-out-methane-can-simply-walk-mordor> [accessed 7 August 2020].

Schulz, Rita, 'WG-PSN Triennial Report 2015-2018', <https://www.iau.org/static/science/scientific_bodies/working_groups/98/wg-psn-triennial-report-2015-2018.pdf> [accessed 7 August 2020].

Stern, S. A. et al., 'The Pluto System: Initial Results from its Exploration by New Horizons', *Science*, 350 (2015), pp. aad1815-1 – 8.

Talbert, Tricia, 'New Horizons Chooses Nickname for "Ultimate" Flyby Target', 13 March 2018 <https://www.nasa.gov/feature/new-horizons-chooses-nickname-for-ultimate-flyby-target> [accessed 7 August 2020].

Tolkien, J.R.R., *The Fellowship of the Ring*, 2nd ed. (Boston: Houghton Mifflin, 1993).
—— *Morgoth's Ring* (Boston: Houghton Mifflin, 1993).
—— *The Return of the King*, 2nd ed. (Boston: Houghton Mifflin, 1993).
—— *The Two Towers*, 2nd ed. (Boston: Houghton Mifflin, 1993).
—— *The Peoples of Middle-earth* (Boston: Houghton Mifflin, 1996).
—— *The Letters of J.R.R. Tolkien* ed. by Christopher Tolkien (Boston: Houghton Mifflin, 2000).
—— *The Silmarillion* (Boston: Houghton Mifflin, 2001).
—— 'The Name "Nodens"', *Tolkien Studies*, 4 (2007), pp. 177-83.

About the Contributors

Cami Agan is a Professor of English in Department of Language and Literature at Oklahoma Christian University. She teaches British Literature with specializations in medieval literature, Tolkien, and drama. She has published on Tolkien, primarily on his First Age materials from *The Silmarillion*, over the last 10 years. Her particular interests in First Age tales center on cultural geography, song-tale-myth, and artifact. She is currently editing a collection entitled *Cities and Strongholds of Middle-earth; Essays on the Habitations in Tolkien's Legendarium* (Mythopoeic Press). For several of her most recent publications, she has used French cultural historian Michel de Certeau's notions of place-space to explore the elegiac resonance of the lost Beleriand.

Marie Bretagnolle is a French doctoral student, currently in her third year. Her work focuses on the illustrations created for British and American editions of Tolkien's Middle-earth texts. She devoted her Master's dissertation to Alan Lee's illustrations for the Centenary edition of The Lord of the Rings and is now preparing her PhD under the joint supervision of Vincent Ferré, a renowned Tolkien specialist (Paris Est-Créteil university), and Isabelle Gadoin, who specialises in text-image relationships (Poitiers university). She has presented her work at Tolkien2019 in Birmingham and, as a specialist of Alan Lee, welcomed and interviewed the artist for the French national Library in February 2020.

Andrew Higgins, PhD is a Tolkien scholar who specialises in exploring the role of language invention in fiction. His thesis 'The Genesis of Tolkien's Mythology' (which he is currently preparing for publication) explored the interrelated nature of myth and language in Tolkien's earliest work. He is also the co-editor with Dr. Dimitra Fimi of *A Secret Vice: Tolkien on Invented Languages* published by HarperCollins in April 2016. Andrew has also taught an online course on language invention for Signum University/Mythgard Institute. He is a trustee of The Tolkien Society, Signum University and is also Director of Development for Imperial War Museums.

Brian Egede-Pedersen is a teacher of History and English at the upper secondary school level, but has also spent three terms as a lecturer at the University of Southern Denmark's History Department. In 2017, he was named Denmark's Teacher of the Year (High School sector), not least for his unorthodox approach to teaching literature, especially fantasy and science fiction. Brian also organizes workshops for other teachers on teaching fantasy and was chosen to introduce the Tolkien (2019) film for one of its only cinematic showings in Denmark. At the 2020 IMC, he will deliver a paper on the appropriations of the Knights Templar in heavy metal.

Mina Lukić obtained her BA and MA degree in Art History at the Faculty of Philosophy of the University of Belgrade. She is currently a PhD student at the same Faculty, specialising in Museology and Heritage Studies, and working on her PhD thesis entitled "Heritage of Fictional Worlds in the Era of Participatory Culture: Modes of Remembering J. R. R. Tolkien's Fictional World". She is employed as a teaching assistant at the Faculty of Philosophy of the University of Pristina in Kosovska Mitrovica.

Kristine Larsen is Professor of Astronomy at Central Connecticut State University. Larsen's work on Tolkien has appeared in *Amon Hen*, *Mallorn*, *Journal of Tolkien Research*, and *Tolkien Studies* (among other journals), and numerous edited collections, including *A Wilderness of Dragons: Essays in Honor of Verlyn Flieger*, *Approaches to Teaching Tolkien's The Lord of the Rings and Other*

Works, Perilous and Fair: Women in the Works and Life of J.R.R. Tolkien, The Hobbit and Tolkien's Mythology, Author of the New Century: T. A. Shippey and the Creation of the Next Canon, and *Tolkien and the Study of His Sources: Critical Essays*.